# Markets and Prosperity

## Edited by

Harry **Stutchbury**

Connor Court Publishing

CONNOR COURT PUBLISHING PTY LTD
PO Box 7257
Redland Bay QLD 4165
sales@connorcourt.com
www.connorcourt.com

Front cover by Ian James

ISBN: 9781922815514

Printed in Australia

# MARKETS & PROSPERITY

EDITED BY

**HARRY STUTCHBURY**

connorcourt

PUBLISHING

For Uncle Darren

# CONTENTS

# Introduction

## Harry Stutchbury

It's not a good time to be an economic rationalist, a small-l liberal, a libertarian, a neo-liberal, a Keating-Labor technocrat, a classical liberal or a small-government conservative. The curves of history have shifted, temporarily at least, away from smaller government and incentive-based policy to paternalistic economic virtue signalling. That's the broad summary of the 17 essays in this collection.

Contributors from both sides of the political aisle, journalists, academics, and business leaders have collectively made the case for the use of markets and incentives to solve some of the major policy challenges we face as a country. These include climate change and energy, childcare, the tax system, the size of government, housing, trade and higher education.

The goal of this collection is twofold. First, to gather the combined input of original thinkers representing the broad swath of the free-market polity in Australia, from centre-left rationalists to libertarian ideologues, and highlight the common thread that aligns them, namely the belief that ceteris paribus, markets are a more efficient tool for the allocation of resources than political decision making. Second, to present challenging and original thinking on our country's problems and how to solve them. Too often, these books can be tired, uninspiring affairs, more likely to have been ripped from a recent media release than represent any original or bold proposal.

The latter is most sharply achieved in Gigi Foster and Paul Frijters' essay. Foster and Frijters take on the political establishment, proposing citizen juries as a tool to appoint senior public servants. This would end political appointments, removing a key cog in the 'favour exchanges' that entrench vested interests in our political economy.

Free-market reform is usually considered through the prism of federal politics as big-ticket items like GST, corporate tax, trade and industrial relations sit under federal jurisdiction. However, most successful reform in the last 15 years has taken place at the state level. Consider the achievements of the New South Wales Coalition Government compared to the federal Coalition Government. Additionally, there is substantial opportunity for reform at the state level. This is why the election of Evan Mulholland and Chris Rath to parliaments in Victoria and New South Wales is encouraging. Mulholland makes the case for a more compassionate approach to criminal justice, easing the burden on the taxpayer and improving people's lives in the process. Rath breaks down a plan to dismantle stamp duty and payroll tax, two viciously inefficient taxes levied at a state level.

No issue has loomed larger over politics in the last 15 years than climate and energy policy. A toxic combination of populism and vested interests has pulled down three prime ministers and resulted in the implementation of a confusing mix of carrots and sticks, instead of a significantly more elegant emissions trading scheme, attempting to lower our carbon emissions while maintaining reliable and affordable energy production. Craig Emerson, Gisele Kapterian and Andrew Bragg outline different market-based solutions to efficiently address this policy trilemma. Given the scope of the energy transition required, and the potential social cost, getting the policy settings right here is crucial.

After climate change, housing policy has the most potential to reshape society and our economy. An economy where the best predictor of your future living standards is how much property your parents bought in metropolitan Sydney or Melbourne 20-plus years ago is not a healthy one. Aaron Patrick outlines the case for increasing housing supply and population density as the only realistic pathway to dealing with this challenge and the political roadblocks and opportunities in the way. Patrick's cutting reminder of the temporal nature of political parties and the potential terminal state of the Liberal Party is particularly compelling.

Childcare is a key driver of financial anxiety for young families. Skyrocketing prices and faltering availability are making it harder for families to make ends meet. Jane Buncle reviews the current state of childcare policy in Australia and identifies potential solutions to improve results for children and parents.

Andrew Low highlights Australia's remarkable economic success off the back of substantial economic reform in the 1980s and 90s and some of the underappreciated features of our economy. However, he is a notable outlier compared to the more pessimistic contributions of Jason Falinski, Gerard Rennick, Tom Switzer and Chaneg Torres, who take a similarly big-picture approach. Falinski outlines the litany of challenges Australia faces and bemoans our political inability to challenge them. Switzer documents the collapse of economic liberalism in the western world and identifies four priorities for policymakers to reverse the trend. Torres details the Liberal Party's descent from small-government liberalism and conservatism to paternalistic populism, charting a course back to majority government that includes embracing the socially conservative and socially progressive sections of the Australian polity. Rennick takes aim at childcare, superannuation and tax policy and the vested interests profiting in a maze of regulation.

Higher education policy is complicated but consequential. Andrew Norton clearly outlines the recent history of higher education reform and the need to balance the social goal of more graduates with the financial constraints. Norton highlights tactical changes to improve outcomes for students and universities.

Protectionism, disguised as industry policy, is in vogue again. Georgina Downer breaks down the legacy of Sir Robert Menzies in dismantling Australia's trade barriers. Nowhere has the political centre of gravity moved more sharply than in trade policy, Downer's essay is a timely reminder that our prosperity hangs on the opening of our economy to competition.

The politics of "spending cuts" has become one of the more pernicious forces in economic policy. Governments are judged on how much they spend on key services, not how well they spend it. Robert Holt proposes a new approach to measuring the effectiveness of government spending. Improving the quality of government spending should be a permanent focus of our political class, not an afterthought. Equipping voters with a framework to evaluate how governments use their tax dollars is a novel approach to doing so.

I used my chapter to tackle the notion that the supposed era of neo-liberal supremacy (the 1980s through to now) has resulted in the hollowing out of the middle class and a fall in real living standards in the west. On the contrary, globalisation has reduced the cost and increased the quality of goods like food, clothing and technology while goods primarily subsidised, distributed or regulated by the government, housing, childcare, and energy, have increased in cost.

History moves quickly. During this book's production, inflation evolved from a 'transitory' concern to an entrenched force at generational highs, leaving central banks scrambling to respond. While it may not be a good political climate for market rationalists, it doesn't change the empirical evidence supporting the superiority of incentives and price signals to government decision-making. It may take sustained stagflation, or another economic crisis, for markets to become du jour again, until then, it's important for the continued development of innovative solutions to our most challenging problems. I hope this collection of essays contributes to that.

*Harry Stutchbury is a Management Consultant at Kearney. He has previously worked as an adviser for Liberal members of parliament and as Deputy Director of the Blueprint Institute.*

# 1

# Australia as a leader in cutting emissions and attracting investment through corporate law

## Andrew Bragg

Why wouldn't Australia look to leverage our position as a world-leading democracy and economy to cut emissions through corporate law and technology? We are a top 20 economy as measured by our G20 status with our nation hitting 12th place in the great gross domestic product (GDP) race.

One of the reasons we are an economic powerhouse is due to our status as a stable, liberal democratic nation with the rule of law and strong public institutions. Our corporate law settings are well-established, reliable and predictable. Australia attracts a large stock of foreign investment and has done so for 250 years.

Despite these strengths, our corporate law is too often static and unresponsive to dynamic changes in the economy. This was noted in various Senate Inquiries into FinTech and digital assets in the 46th Parliament. Only in February 2022 was the requirement for so-called 'wet signatures' and paper-based execution of documents removed, 20 years after the passing of the Corporations Act.

Australia should be using corporate law to attract new investment and achieve important economic objectives to a much greater degree. There is much to learn from Singapore in this respect. Emissions reduction is one of these important economic objectives.

There are three key areas of corporate law we should deploy to cut emissions and improve our dynamism.

One key area we need to lead on is emissions disclosure. If we move quickly to implement local laws to require emissions to be publicly disclosed, economic risk will be clearer and investment should be easier to attract.

The second is achieving first mover advantage on digital assets laws, by passing a set of laws that protect consumers but also promote investment in Australia.

The third key area is ensuring emissions reduction (carbon credit) units can be easily tokenised and traded.

The emissions disclosure and digital asset laws provide the framework and basis for achieving the reduction of carbon emissions. The latter is facilitated by these two baseline elements.

*The Economic Imperative of Net Zero*

Our commitment to net zero emissions has been well and truly flagged. As a nation, we can all win from net zero. I am proud that the Liberal Government committed Australia to net zero emissions in 2021.

I have long seen climate risk as an economic risk. I said in 2015:

> The concepts underpinning traditional investment methodology apply equally to all matters of environmental, social and governance (ESG) risk factors. An environmental or social externality will generally have an economic cost. Therefore, issues surrounding fossil fuels... should be considered through an economic lens.

Net zero is more than an environmental objective. It is a critical economic imperative for our nation. I have been heavily influenced by the work of Professor Alan Finkel. In his essay, *Getting to Net Zero*, Finkel says that Australia can significantly cut out total emissions by tripling solar and wind energy production to replace fossil fuels.

There will still be emissions from things like cement production and farming. But the emissions need to be eaten by soil carbon or Direct Air Capture. Australia should have a unique carbon capture advantage given our land mass.

The strength of Finkel's work is that it breaks down the emissions challenge into bite-size chunks. He shows the path forward and how it can be achieved. We can overcome the emissions challenge through the broader use of existing emerging technologies.

The Liberal Party committed Australia to net zero emissions at the Glasgow Conference of the Parties (COP) in 2021 and established Australia as a leader in low-emissions technologies.

We are proud of this commitment and I believe we can go further by revising our targets in the interceding years to 2050. Based on Finkel's work, it is clear we can get a deeper cut by 2030 of at least 40% on 2005 levels.

Independent consultancy Climate Analytics estimates the Australian states alone will deliver a 34% cut through their actions, as seen in the state of New South Wales.

There are many opportunities for the Commonwealth in emissions disclosure and corporate law reform that will provide a great economic and environmental benefit to Australia, while also drawing on Australia's core equities as a sophisticated, high-wage economy.

We have already seen new-generation technologies drive growth in energy and the race to net zero. Solar energy is being exported around the globe by the giant Sun Cable development, to capitalise on Australia's great natural endowment of resources.

FinTech companies are powering the clean energy transition for consumers. Buy Now Pay Later firm Brighte estimates that in 2021, 15-20% of all solar installations were financed by BNPL. This new technology-enabled consumers to overcome the upfront cost of clean energy.

In October 2022, South Australia became the first major jurisdiction globally to fuel 100% of its total energy demand through solar, from noon to 1:00 pm. Former CEO of the Australian Energy Market Operator, Audrey Zibelman, said: "Never before has a jurisdiction the size of South Australia been completely run by solar power".

Australia has demonstrated its capacity to be a world leader in this space. One key focus for the government is in identifying and facilitating the capital needed to fund the journey to net zero.

To achieve this objective, the government needs to set out a detailed policy programme to give the markets certainty. The government needs to create a regulatory environment that will appropriately harness new technology and welcome investment.

The key question is: how much will it cost the nation to get to net zero emissions? There is, of course, a cost to replacing existing energy-generating assets. The costs of decarbonisation of energy, transport and industry need to be considered clearly as they are quite separate tasks.

It is possible that Australia has not thought carefully enough about these costs. The Department of Climate Change, Energy, the Environment and Water and the Treasury has not provided a clear answer on the capital cost for Australia's transition in response to questions when the Senate inquired into 2022 emissions reduction target legislation.

According to the Australian National University's Professor Frank Jotzo:

> To my knowledge, no comprehensive and authoritative estimate for Australia is available. But it must be said that the IEA [International Energy Agency] does not place a particular emphasis on Australia as one country—or, should we say, continent. This actually goes to a broader point of the need to strengthen the capacity and capability in Australia to provide very detailed analysis on the technological and economic aspects of this transition.

We do know that the transition to net zero will be incredibly expensive. It is estimated that annual private investment will need to be 8 times its current level by 2030, to support the clean energy transition.

The Business Council of Australia (BCA) have referred to Finkel's 2017 estimation that $890 billion will be required to be spent on "power generation, transmission and distribution by 2050 to meet our net zero target."

The BCA expects that other sectors will require similarly large levels of investment.

The Investor Group on Climate Change (IGCC) wrote in 2020 about the medium-term value of investment needed in each sector:

> Investment in renewable and clean electricity production through the period 2020 to 2050 is the sector that will emerge as the largest investment opportunity overall ($385 billion). After 2030, commercial-scale opportunities in green hydrogen production hit scale, leading to substantial investment in the emerging industry. By 2050, green hydrogen is the second-largest investment opportunity at nearly $350 billion. The next largest opportunities to 2050 are transport infrastructure ($104 billion), carbon sequestration ($102 billion), and electricity transmission and distribution ($98 billion).

Much of this capital will need to come from overseas, as Australia has rarely had enough capital to fund our investment needs. I am optimistic about our national net zero economy, but we cannot gloss over the challenges. That is not leadership.

Strong policies should be designed to reduce emissions in energy, transport and industry, for example, while supporting the broader uptake of existing technologies. Other policies could include transmission initiatives and greater emphasis on externality reduction through tax policies.

This is the core framework that is required to drive emissions reduction. The following policy ideas can build on the decarbonisation agenda that Australia needs.

*Corporate Law: Leading on Carbon Disclosure*

One key policy that Australia should adopt is a carbon reporting mechanism with an aggressive timetable. A mechanism like this would ensure that Australian companies would have a first-mover advantage in disclosing their risk profile.

I believe the Australian Parliament should pass laws that require organisations to disclose their emissions across all three of the 'emissions scopes'.

Australia should be a leader in carbon disclosure. A firm carbon disclosure regime would not only improve transparency but also attract marginal capital. If you are an international investor, a disclosure regime will allow you to look into an organisation and assess its risk profile according to its scope 1, 2 and 3 emissions.

Scope 1 greenhouse gas emissions as those directly produced from a company's activities. Scope 2 emissions are generated indirectly through the consumption of an energy commodity, such as electricity, heat or cooling. Scope 3 emissions cover all indirect emissions generated in the economy.

Under the current regime, scope 3 emissions are not reported. This category captures emissions created as a consequence of a company's activities, but from sources not owned or controlled by that company.

The International Sustainability Standards Board published draft *International Financial Reporting Sustainability Disclosure Standards* in March 2022.

In the exposure draft, the ISSB wrote:

> An entity shall disclose information that enables users of general purpose financial reporting to understand the effects of significant climate-related risks and opportunities on its financial position, financial performance and cash flows for the reporting period, and the anticipated effects over the short, medium and long term — including how climate-related risks and opportunities are included in the entity's financial planning. An entity shall disclose quantitative information unless it is unable to do so. If an entity is unable to provide quantitative information, it shall provide qualitative information. When providing quantitative information, an entity can disclose single amounts or a range.

Providing investors with this level of transparency and certainty about Australian companies will, I believe, encourage them to place their investments in our businesses, rather than in other jurisdictions with less fulsome disclosure requirements.

We should not simply be encouraging self-regulated carbon disclosure. We should not be asking the Corporate Governance Council to publish a note.

The Investor Group on Climate Change provided testimony to the Senate in 2022 on the need for Australia to put in reporting mechanisms for companies that deal with scope 1, 2 & 3 emissions, in line with the ISSB global standards:

> I think we have the advantage that some of the work is actually being done for us internationally through the International Sustainability Standards Board, which is establishing global standards, which is actually really important for investors because

the last thing we want is market fragmentation, with different standards in lots of different countries... The whole point is setting the parameters so business can prepare. At the moment, we're in a situation where there's uncertainty in the market about when it's going to happen.

The Financial Services Council has also called for a mandatory climate disclosure regime to be developed:

> We want a mandatory climate disclosure regime, and we've called for that and think that is a priority. But it should be a principle-based regime; it shouldn't be overly prescriptive.

This year, the Commonwealth Bank of Australia ('CBA') became the first Australian bank to disclose its financed scope 3 emissions.

CBA disclosed figures that were much higher than previously expected, stressing the extent of the hidden carbon risks faced by customers and the market. The Financial Review reported that:

> CBA's historic disclosure last month was eye-opening because banks' scope 3 emissions were previously thought to be around 700 times larger than scope 1. Emmi estimates CBA scope 1 emissions for 2021 were 10,600 tonnes – making scope 3 larger by 2300 times.

At the moment, other Australian organisations have no obligation to follow in CBA's footsteps. According to the exposure draft of the ISSB global standards published this year, organisations would be required to make disclosures about their sustainability-related risks and opportunities.

These disclosures would include the organisation's strategy or transition plans for addressing those risks and opportunities, and the organisation's metrics and targets for monitoring its performance. The disclosures would have scope to capture important information about how climate risks will affect an organisation's cash flow and long-term business strategy.

New Zealand has already passed laws to require disclosures, their External Reporting Board said:

> For financial institutions included in the regime, this will mean measuring the financial emissions of a portfolio. This enables financial institutions to set targets, inform actions and disclose progress. Understanding these emissions is crucial for portfolio alignment and decarbonisation.

The United States has set out expectations in draft Securities Exchange Commission guidance, saying:

> A registrant would be required to disclose GHG emissions from upstream and downstream activities in its value chain (Scope 3), if material or if the registrant has set a GHG emissions target or goal that includes Scope 3 emissions.

Given our competitors are already moving, we will need legal requirements to give Australian businesses and investors the necessary level of certainty.

Given the ISSB global standards are virtually finalised, Australia should start the process of implementing them domestically. At the time of writing, the Australian Treasury is consulting on a proposal to introduce carbon disclosure for the financial year 2024-25.

We should be looking to introduce a voluntary approach for companies wanting to move quickly in 2023-24. The faster we move on disclosure, the easier it will be to attract capital and smooth the decarbonisation transition.

*The tokenisation of Carbon Credits*

The implementation of a carbon disclosure regime could be backed by embracing digital assets innovation and deploying a modern system for carbon credits.

The idea that only the wealthiest fund managers with wholesale access to an obscure system should be able to win exposure to emissions reduction is un-Australian.

The truth is there is no easy way for Australian workers to gain easy exposure to emissions reduction units. It is the preserve of the wealthy.

The Australian system was established in 2009. Law firm Corrs Chambers Westgarth describe the system as:

> ACCUs are created and issued under the Carbon Credits (Carbon Farming Initiative) Act 2011 (Cth) ('CFI Act'). Each ACCU represents one tonne of carbon dioxide that is abated through an eligible offsets project (being a project which avoids the emission of greenhouse gases or removes them from the atmosphere).

The Clean Energy Regulator (CER) says:

> The Australian National Registry of Emissions Units (ANREU) is administered by the Clean Energy Regulator. ANREU is a system designed to meet one of Australia's commitments under the Kyoto Protocol. The Protocol requires each country with an emission reduction target to establish a national registry to ensure accurate accounting of the issuance, holding, transfer, acquisition, cancellation, retirement and carry-over of Kyoto units.

The only way to trade these units is to have an account with ANREU which can take up to six months to obtain according to industry sources.

An ACCU is a unit issued to an eligible person by the CER

under section 147 of the CFI Act. The ACCU is created by making an entry for the unit in an account kept by the person in the electronic ANREU.

From a tax perspective, ACCUs are subject to a unique Australian tax law (division 420). This law effectively forces holders of units to take them to account at the end of the financial year. This means that holders are potentially liable to a tax obligation regardless of whether the units have been sold or traded. It is therefore effectively treated as an income set and not a CGT asset.

BetaCarbon is one market player which has gone to the trouble of obtaining a licence to trade. It has then tokenised its credits to create an alternative secondary market. In doing so it predicts the average trade in Australia will go from $100,000 to $1.

Betacarbon "has minted tokens covering 93,000 tonnes of carbon drawing from 32 emissions reduction projects ranging from landfill gas, native forest regeneration, and indigenous savanna burning."

One of its backers, former ASIC Deputy Chair Dan Crennan says:

> The ACCU system, which is more or less consistent with carbon credit systems, was designed some time ago and designed seemingly for a small group of participants and industries that were obligated to participate in the decarbonisation system; In other words large-scale miners and polluters.

It shouldn't be this hard. There is no need to use a bespoke unit registry system or to unnecessarily restrict access to trading.

An Independent Review was completed by the Albanese

government into Carbon Credit Units, led by Professor Ian Chubb AC.

> The purpose of the Review is to ensure that ACCUs and Australia's carbon crediting framework are strong and credible and will be supported by participants, purchasers and the broader community.

The Review said the scheme is fundamentally sound but it put forward several recommendations.

> The Panel makes a number of recommendations. The purpose of each is to improve the scheme: to clarify intention where necessary; to clearly identify (and separate) the key roles of integrity assurance, regulation and administration; to remove unnecessary restrictions on data sharing; to enable free prior and informed consent; and to improve information and incentives, including in relation to non-carbon benefits and attributes.

As part of the response to the review, Australia should look to establish a world-leading carbon credits tokenisation system to broaden the mandate of the scheme. We should also do it to protect the scheme's integrity.

Blockchain is a natural partner for cutting emissions. The European Union has written:

> Blockchain is a powerful tool that can significantly improve the transparency, accountability and traceability of greenhouse gas emissions. It helps companies provide more accurate, reliable, standardised, and readily available data on carbon emissions...

> Blockchain can be utilised through smart contracts to better calculate, track and report on the reduction of the carbon footprint across the entire value chain. It can provide instant authentication, verification of real-time data and clear data records.

Within the short lifespan of digital assets, the ACCU regime was established a lifetime ago. The rules are prescriptive, novel and unsuited for broader trading purposes.

If we want to provide democratic access to carbon credit units, a significant body of law reform is needed to mainstream the credit units as interoperable.

## Regulate Tokens

Facilitating the tokenisation of carbon credit units is only half the battle. The second half of the battle is ensuring digital assets themselves are regulated properly.

20% of the population has owned some form of crypto. Australia is in a race for consumer protection, capital attraction and innovation. Instead of taking fast action to respond to existing Treasury consultations on crypto markets and custody, the current government has commissioned another review. Our competitors are enhancing their regulatory systems while we establish endless reviews.

The recommendations of the Senate Select Committee on Australia as a Financial and Technology Centre published in October 2021 stacked up internationally. The recommendations were largely similar to the executive order made by United States President Joe Biden in March 2022, after our recommendations were released.

Other jurisdictions are striking ahead. In the United States, Senators Lummis and Gillibrand are working to pass the Responsible Financial Innovation Act. This Act would provide a comprehensive set of regulations for the digital assets market, where the Commodity Futures Trading Commission would regulate digital commodities, stablecoin and other assets.

This is not only a race for capital and investment in this industry but a race for our country's future and economy.

As a result of the Labor Government's failure to progress in this agenda, I have taken it upon myself to develop a Private Member's Bill: the *Digital Assets (Market Regulation) Bill 2022* ('Digital Assets Bill').

Australians currently face a gaping hole in the regulatory framework. Investment in a financial product is protected, while investment in a crypto product is not.

Further exacerbating this issue is Australia's licensing framework. Crypto providers hold financial services licenses, not licenses specifically for crypto products. This gives the impression that these providers are offering a regulated product when they are not.

To address this regulatory hole, my Digital Assets Bill includes a licensing regime with the following three licence categories:

1. Digital Asset Exchange

2. Digital Asset Custodian

3. Stablecoin Issuer

This regime has a twofold rationale.

First, by providing a standards-based regime, consumers can have confidence that risk exposure is managed, and on par with other financial services and products.

Second, by providing regulatory certainty, the door to greater investment and growth in Australia's crypto ecosystem and the virtual economy is opened.

This can be achieved with licensee provisions. I have proposed the following:

- Minimum capital requirements (s 10(2)(a))

- Conduct regulation, and appropriate governance of user activity monitoring and procedures. This brings the industry out of the wild-west situation in which it currently resides (ss 10(2)(b)-(c))

- Segregation of customer funds, to ensure that customer money is not tied up with corporate funds if a digital currency exchange or custody service declares bankruptcy (s 10(2)(d))

- Cybersecurity requirements, setting industry standards to protect consumers from the threat of crypto exchange hacks (s 10(2)(e)

- Requirements for key personnel responsible for digital asset custody services to be based in Australia (s 14(2)(a))

- Disclosure requirements to both participants and government agencies (ss 10(2)(f), (h))

To ensure that the parliament leads these reforms and regulators are not running the show, the Minister would have the responsibility for issuing licences. ASIC would have the responsibility of administering and enforcing the regime and will be granted monitoring and investigative authority.

This industry must come out of the shadows and into the light.

The Digital Assets Bill provides for a transition period as the industry progresses.

The Bill also sets out a regulatory framework for firms issuing stablecoins.

In the recent collapse of algorithmic stablecoin, Terra, an estimated $60 billion went up in smoke in a 'digital run'.

Minimum reserve standards must be introduced to ensure that stablecoin issuers provide consumers with a reasonable standard of consumer protection.

In reference to stablecoins, the Governor of the Reserve Bank of Australia, Philip Lowe, said that it is "important that these tokens are backed by high-quality assets and that they meet high standards for safety and security." Translation: the Australian Parliament should legislate to protect consumers.

In a similar vein, United States Treasury Secretary, Janet Yellen, has urged lawmakers to move on consumer protection in the digital race.

It is with this in mind that the Bill contains provisions requiring licensees to hold in reserve the full amount of the face value of liabilities on the issue in the form of Australian legal tender or foreign equivalent. The stablecoin issuer must hold the capital in an Australian bank to satisfy its licence obligations.

The Lummis-Gillibrand Bill provides a useful precedent, underlining the importance of international collaboration in setting global regulatory standards.

Stablecoins could be a solution to the eye-watering problem faced by 1.7 billion people: de-banking. Unfortunately, there are as many risks as there are opportunities when it comes to stablecoins.

In summary, Australia should build on our net zero commitment by aggressively pursuing three sets of corporate and financial law reform:

1. Corporate emissions disclosure;

2. Democratise carbon credit exposure; and

3. Regulate digital assets.

These are the decarbonisation issues upon which we Liberals must lead.

> *Andrew Bragg is a Senator representing New South Wales in the Parliament of Australia. He previously worked in financial services.*

# 2

# Revitalising the Australian childcare sector: The role of federation reform

## Jane Buncle

Childcare is an essential service that allows parents to balance work and family responsibilities, while also supporting the development and education of young children. In Australia, childcare has become increasingly important as more parents enter the workforce and rely on childcare services to care for their children. Childcare is also an important factor in the strength of the Australian economy, contributing to workforce participation, economic stimulus, future workforce development, and gender equality. However, the childcare system in Australia is facing challenges, including high costs, burdensome regulation, limited availability, and uneven quality. These challenges have significant implications for families, the workforce, and the broader economy.

In this essay, I will argue that reform to federation in Australia has the potential to make the childcare industry more efficient by reducing duplication and fragmentation in the sector. Currently, the childcare industry is subject to a complex web of regulations, funding arrangements, and governance structures across different states and territories. This can create inefficiencies and redundancies in service delivery, as well as confusion for families seeking affordable and high-quality care. Federation reform could help to address these issues by creating a more streamlined and coordinated approach to governance and service delivery. By creating a more efficient and consistent childcare sector, federation reform could help to improve cost and availability outcomes for children and families, while also ensuring that resources are used more effectively and efficiently.

*Childcare in Australia today*

There are several types of childcare provided in Australia, including long day care, family day care, outside school hours care, occasional care and community preschools. While the availability of these types of care may vary depending on location and demand, long day care remains the primary choice for Australian parents seeking childcare services. This type of care provides full-day care for children from infancy to school age, typically from around 7 am to 6 pm. Long day care is a popular choice for working parents who require full-time care for their children, as it provides a structured environment with trained staff who can support children's development and education.

Responsibility for childcare is shared between federal, state and territory governments. The federal government is primarily responsible for the regulation and funding of childcare services, including the development of national quality standards and the provision of financial support to families and providers. The regulatory framework is overseen by the Department of Education and Training and the Australian Children's Education & Care Quality Authority, which is responsible for setting national quality standards for childcare services.[1] The state and territory governments are responsible for the delivery and oversight of childcare services within their respective jurisdictions, including the licensing and regulation of providers, and the provision of subsidies to families to help cover the cost of care.

Funding is provided through a combination of government subsidies and private fees. These fees vary depending on the type of childcare, the location, and the quality of the service. Childcare providers may also receive funding from state and territory governments, grants and donations, and fundraising activities.

The federal government provides several types of subsidies to assist families with the cost of childcare. These subsidies are income-tested and can help to reduce the cost of childcare for eligible families. The main form of government subsidy for childcare in Australia is the Childcare Subsidy (CCS). This is available to families to help cover the cost of long day care. The subsidy is paid directly to the childcare provider, and the amount of subsidy a family receives depends on their income, the type of childcare they use, and the hours of care they need.[2]

---

1   Education and Care Services National Law and the Education and Care Services National Regulations.
2   Others include the Additional Childcare Subsidy, which is available to families in financial hardship or with additional needs; The other is the Jobs, Education

*What are the challenges posed to the Australian childcare sector?*

The Australian childcare industry has faced challenges for many years, but they centre upon a lack of affordability and accessibility. Research has consistently identified several factors that are contributing to this, which can be summarised as follows:

1.  Wages are the largest cost for childcare providers, and they have been increasing over time. Early childhood educators are highly trained professionals, and they are in high demand. As such, they command higher wages than in the past. This has led to an increase in the cost of providing childcare services.

2.  The regulation of the childcare industry has become more stringent over time, which has increased the cost of compliance for childcare providers. For example, there are now more staff-to-child ratios and higher qualification requirements for early childhood educators. These requirements are important for ensuring high-quality care, but they also increase the cost of providing childcare services.

3.  Childcare providers face other operating costs, including rent, utilities, insurance, and supplies. These costs can be impacted by inflation, changes in government policy, and other factors.

4.  The demand for childcare services has been increasing over time, which has put upward pressure on prices. This is due in part to changes in workforce participation patterns, with more parents working than in the past.

Inflation is also having a significant impact on the cost of childcare because as the cost of living increases, so does the cost of providing childcare, as childcare providers may need to pay more for supplies, wages, and other expenses. This is leading to higher fees for families and it is making it more difficult for them to afford high-quality childcare. In addition,

---

and Training Childcare Fee assistance, which is available to parents who are studying or training.

inflation is also impacting the purchasing power of families, as their income is not keeping pace with the rising cost of living. This is making it even more difficult for families to afford childcare and is contributing to a growing affordability gap in the childcare industry.

To address these challenges, many believe that the solution is to put forward policies that support the affordability of childcare through higher subsidies. The exact cost invested by the federal and state governments varies from year to year — depending on factors such as the number of children using childcare services and changes to government policy — but the amount is increasing. The provision of the CCS is projected to cost the budget $63 Billion over the next decade.

There is no doubt that funding is an important tool to mitigate the cost of childcare and the cost of childcare subsidies like the CCS is partially offset by revenue from taxes, as many families who receive subsidies are working and paying income tax. But the effect of the subsidy has very likely contributed to an increase in the cost of childcare due to increased demand that is not presently being met by enough supply to meet that demand. Further, despite the increased funding, complaints about the inconsistency and lack of availability of childcare in Australia are also increasing.

Families and providers across Australia cite issues such as varying quality standards, regulations, and funding arrangements across different states and territories. This inconsistency is leading to confusion, inequity, and frustration for families and providers seeking high-quality and reliable childcare. Additionally, the inconsistency in the availability of childcare services is creating challenges for families seeking to balance work and family responsibilities. This is demonstrated by the fact that 9 million Australians (35.2% of the population) have no access to childcare at all, which is a problem particularly faced by Australians in rural and regional areas.[3]

One of the main drivers of the lack of accessibility and affordability is how childcare is regulated and funded in Australia. As described above, the childcare industry in Australia is currently regulated by a range of federal and state laws, regulations, and standards. This multi-layered approach means there is a lack of centralised accountability for the provision of childcare services amongst federal and state governments, whilst entrenching inflexible government policy to meet the growing problems in this sector.

This multilayered regulation also places a significant burden on childcare providers, leading to higher costs that are passed on to families in the form of higher fees. It is also limiting innovation in the industry by imposing strict guidelines that may not be flexible enough to accommodate new and emerging models of childcare in particular areas of Australia. Further, the regulatory framework is creating barriers to entry for new providers, making it difficult for smaller operators to enter the market and compete with larger providers.

The net result is a loss to Australian children and families. For this reason, as we go on it is important that we strike a balance between protecting children and families and promoting innovation and competition in the industry.

---

3     Hurley, P., Matthews, H., & Pennicuik, S. (2022). *Deserts and oases: How accessible is childcare?* Mitchell Institute, Victoria University pg 4.

## What are the solutions to these challenges?

There is broad recognition that the childcare industry in Australia is broken and requires urgent reform. At the time of writing, the Albanese Government has commissioned the Australian Competition and Consumer Commission (ACCC) and the Productivity Commission to come up with possible solutions to some of these problems, with those findings due to be handed down in November 2023.

The solution to these problems requires more than tinkering at the edges of policy. It will demand bold reform across the sector and the whole of government. The first step in this approach would be to reform the federation so that state governments are given responsibility for childcare. This could create a more cohesive, cost-effective and coordinated approach to childcare, which could improve the quality and accessibility of childcare services and benefit both children and families. The reasons for this are as follows.

First, it would allow for decisions to be made at a more local level, accounting for the specific needs and circumstances of each state. State governments could use their local knowledge to develop more tailored solutions to the specific needs of their communities such as providing direct incentives to childcare providers to encourage them to locate in areas where there is a shortage of childcare services. This could help to address issues such as the shortage of childcare places in regional and rural areas in what has become known as 'childcare deserts'. This would reflect the fact that states are better able to align their childcare policies and funding within their broader social and economic priorities in a way that differs from national priorities.

Second, it would enable more accountability for the quality of educational outcomes for children within their borders from end to end and provide a greater incentive for them to invest in high-quality childcare services. Enabling states to be responsible for education from end to end fits with the concept of the states having full control over all aspects of education, from early childhood education to tertiary education. This model of education governance has many benefits:

1. It allows for a more coordinated and integrated approach to education. With the states having full control over all levels of education, they can ensure that there is a clear progression from early childhood education to primary and secondary education, and then on to tertiary education. This can help to ensure that students receive a consistent and coherent education experience and that there is a smooth transition between different levels of education.

2. It can allow for greater flexibility and responsiveness to local needs and priorities. With the states having full control over education, they can tailor education policies and programs to meet the specific needs and priorities of their communities. For example, schools could play a key role in providing childcare services, particularly in areas where there are limited options, and can work to expand the role of schools in childcare by providing funding and support for school-based childcare programs. This can help to ensure that education is relevant and responsive to local contexts.

Third, it would enhance and incentivise innovation in the sector. Incentivising innovation is an important way to promote the development of new and improved childcare services and states are better placed to experiment with new approaches to childcare and early childhood education given their localised knowledge. One example of how this can be achieved is through funding mechanisms that reward innovative practices and approaches. For instance, the government could offer grants or tax incentives to childcare providers who implement innovative programs that improve outcomes for children and families. Another example is the creation of collaborative networks and knowledge-sharing platforms that encourage providers to share best practices and learn from each other. These types of incentives can help to spur innovation and improvements in the childcare sector, ultimately leading to better outcomes for children and families. State governments are already recognising the role they play in innovating the sector, with the Perrottet Government and Andrews Government in Victoria and New South Wales announcing a landmark policy whereby every family in either state will have access to a full year of free quality preschool education for their children by 2030.

Fourth, in relation to funding, federation reform could also help to address the issue of funding for childcare services. As described above, the federal government currently provides funding for childcare primarily through the CCS. However, the distribution of funding can be complex and uneven, which can make it difficult for childcare providers to access the resources they need. Reform to federation could create a more streamlined and coordinated funding model for childcare that could help to ensure that funding is distributed more fairly and efficiently among the states where there are higher populations and higher demand for these services. This could also help to boost the supply of child-care places and make childcare more affordable for families across the country.

Overall, there are many benefits to giving states more control over childcare in Australia. While greater state control could lead to more tailored solutions and better coordination, critics will no doubt suggest that it could also create inconsistencies and fragmentation, as well as challenges around funding and resource allocation. It will also require the federal and state governments to start a brave conversation about the distribution of revenue among the states to support the growing budgetary demand for these services. Ultimately, any changes to the distribution of responsibilities and funding in the childcare system will need to be carefully considered to ensure that they benefit children and families across the country.

*Jane Buncle is a Sydney based Barrister specialising in commercial matters, royal commissions and international commercial arbitrations.*

# 3

# Menzies and Free Trade: Lessons for Today

## Georgina Downer

*Introduction*

Australia's longest-serving Prime Minister, Robert Gordon Menzies, is not renowned as one of history's great economic reformers. Education, ANZUS, immigration, yes, but on the economy, the narrative that is often spun claims that the Menzies years fortuitously benefitted from the post-war boom times. So, it supposedly follows that post-War population growth and other lucky circumstances – rather than economic strategies of the Menzies era – generated low unemployment, and wage growth and prosperity.

Although that narrative sits well with the folklore of Australia as a lucky country, it misses a key economic contribution of the Prime Ministership of Robert Menzies. This essay highlights that the Menzies era marks the beginning of an important shift in Australia's trade policy and market orientation. In the face of significant opposition, it was under Menzies in the 1950s that Australia recognised the economic imperative and geopolitical advantage of trade with Asia. Beginning with the 1957 Commerce Agreement with Japan, Menzies demonstrated the importance of finding new markets, pushing back against vested interests, and taking the long view. While Menzies retained much of the protectionist architecture of his predecessor Alfred Deakin's Liberals, his rhetoric marked a shifting realisation that Australia's future prosperity would require an economy based on free enterprise, open markets, and foreign investment.

In this way, Menzies laid the foundations for economic growth and the ongoing trade and economic liberalisation that followed. The liberalising reforms of the 1980s and 1990s and the raft of free trade agreements of the 2000s have continued Australia's stellar economic record. Now, in the face of rising protectionism and an increasingly mercurial global economy, Australia's liberal trade policy settings present risks to its prosperity. We should look back at the Menzies era and remember the importance of taking the long view and finding new markets and opportunities for trade. We need to, like Menzies, respond to geopolitical trends as we find them, adopt new geoeconomic strategies to deal with increasing strategic competition, and push back against the vested interests that make difficult policy choices even more so.

*Menzies Redux*

On 10 December 1949, Menzies led his youthful Liberal Party to its first electoral victory, becoming Prime Minister for the second time. Of the staggering 50 new Coalition members elected in 1949, 34 had served in World War Two. Animosity towards Japan continued to run high as stories of atrocities committed by the Japanese Imperial forces against Australians circulated throughout the country.

Menzies had already made clear his intention to move beyond wartime animosity and towards peace and reconciliation with Japan. As early as 1942, in his radio broadcast on 'Hatred as an Instrument of War Policy', Menzies said,

> "if this war with all its tragedy breeds into us a deep-seated and enduring spirit of hatred, then the peace when it comes will be merely the prelude to disaster and not an end of it. ... Peace must not only close the door on war; it must open the door to better things."

Coming to power in 1949, the Menzies government's focus was on post-war reconstruction. Menzies saw in Australia the potential to be a significant country, distinct from Britain, with a prosperous economy and educated middle class. To do this Australia needed a bigger population and to foster the rapid development of industries. The 1950s and 60s were, as the economist Henry Ergas puts it, "a golden age of Australian economic growth."[4] Between 1950 and 1965, Australia's annual growth rate was 4.1%, the population grew by almost 40% (from 8.3 million to 11.5 million), and unemployment stayed around 3%. Jobs for new Australians were plentiful, and the good times were rolling.

*Australia's future lies with Japan*

Menzies and his Trade Minister John McEwen recognised that a key component of Australia's trade and strategic future lay with a prosperous and peaceful Japan. For Japan to reach its potential as a significant Pacific power, both in influence and economy, it would need trade partners like Australia which

---

4    Ergas, H and Pincus, J.J. 2016.

produced many of the commodities that an industrialising Japan would need (namely wool and minerals). Additionally, although Australia had plentiful natural resources, it had a relative shortage of domestic capital and so needed to attract international investment to fund ground-breaking resources projects. Shutting Japan out of trade, investment and regional engagements could leave it exposed to the influences of global communism or even allow militarism to take hold once again. The future of Japan concerned Allied efforts to shape the region so much so that the founder of the CIA, Bill Donovan, wrote to Australia's Minister for External Affairs Richard Casey, urging the development of Australia's coal mines to provide Japan with much-needed energy supplies. Not only would this assist the Japanese in their much-needed post-war industrialisation, but it would also dissuade Japan from purchasing coal from China and the USSR, thus potentially falling into the arms of global communism. Menzies's vision was prescient. Japan is Australia's second-largest export market at $46.4 billion in 2020 (10.6 per cent of total exports, comprised of natural gas ($14.2 billion) and coal at $11.7 billion).[5]

Menzies was also concerned that to defend itself from threats from abroad, Japan needed to be successful and independent. Menzies was aware that leaving Japan weakened could mean the United States and its allies would need to prop it up indefinitely.

Another concern for Menzies was how to mitigate the risk for Australian exporters of losing the British market. Menzies could see Britain moving closer to joining the Common Market

---

5    Statistics from Department of Foreign Affairs, Japan Country Brief, 2022.

of the European Economic Community. Once this happened, Australia would lose an important market for its agricultural produce. Australia's trade at that time was mainly with Britain and its dominions, which before the General Agreement on Tariffs and Trade had been attractive under the Imperial Preference arrangements. Together, Australia's exports to Britain and the Commonwealth amounted to over 60% of all its exports in 1948-49. This figure plunged to just 34% by the end of the Menzies era in 1966. Conversely, exports to Asia almost tripled during that period, rising from 6.5% to 16.8%.

## The fight against vested interests

Even before founding the Liberal Party in 1944, Menzies had railed against the toxic influence of vested interests in politics. He had resigned as Minister without portfolio in 1929 on a matter of principle, refusing to support the Victorian government of Sir William McPherson successively underwriting a poorly run business at the behest of the Country Progressive Party. Menzies believed it wasn't good enough for politicians merely to manage a country according to the whims of business lobbies, pressure groups or organised labour; they must do so according to a set of guiding principles. Sick of politics dominated by pressure groups, Menzies's Liberal Party was established by a set of individuals, not organisations or businesses, committed to a defined philosophy, and deliberately designed to minimise the pressure of vested interests.

When it came to tackling protectionism, the biggest challenge for Menzies was the Australian manufacturing industry, predominantly located in Menzies's home state of Victoria. Australia was, after New Zealand, the most protected economy in the world during the 20th century. Menzies recognised the politics of protectionism was murderously tricky to navigate, but that Australia's future lay with a strong export-driven economy given our agricultural potential, natural resources and small population.

Even as early as 1942, Menzies recognised that the world was moving in the United States-led direction of trade liberalisation and that Australia would have to be ready for this:

> "We in Australia should not take these things for granted. We should prepare our minds to understand that while the development of the industrial resources of Australia is something dear to our hearts and, as we think, good for everybody, we cannot expect when the war is over to live in a little watertight compartment of our own."

While he was no Reidite free trader, in government Menzies was, as David Kemp has argued, 'prepared to let protection erode and come under challenge'. He recognised that Australia's economy 'rested upon our great exports and upon the willingness of foreign countries to buy them'. Without trade, Australia would not prosper and grow.

### Leading trade with Japan

Ceding some protectionist policies would be necessary for Australia to increase its exports to Japan. This became the inspiration for the Commerce Agreement with Japan, with negotiations starting in October 1956 and the Agreement swiftly signed in July 1957. The Agreement would relax Australia's tariffs on Japanese goods in exchange for expanding

Australia's exports to Japan (at that time, mainly wool and wheat). The Agreement would improve the balance of trade for Japan, although it would remain in Australia's favour.

With the prospect of an influx of Japanese imports due to the Commerce Agreement, Menzies and McEwen's intentions didn't necessarily correspond with those of the Australian people. Menzies remarked in his memoirs 'A Measure of the Years' of the 'hostility in Australia, among both manufacturers and the general public, to the making of any special agreement with Japan which might increase Japanese exports to Australia'.

Public animosity towards Japan in the 1950s remained strong, with many experiencing firsthand the atrocities of Japanese soldiers during the war. Japanese products were viewed by many Australians as low quality, produced by cheap labour, and designed to undercut Australian-made goods.

As expected, the scare campaign against the Commerce Agreement was significant. The Associated Chamber of Manufacturers called the Agreement a "blueprint for unemployment", while Crunda Knitting Mills put a full-page advertisement in the Sydney Morning Herald with a banner reading "UNEMPLOYMENT – It's up to you, Mr Menzies". The ACTU collected 30,000 signatures from employees in the clothing and textiles industry who opposed the Agreement, while 5000 union members marched through Sydney in protest.

The opposition Labor Party strongly opposed the Agreement with Opposition leader Dr H V Evatt labelling it a form of "economic aggression", while his firebrand colleague Eddie Ward said it was a "criminal action against the Australian nation".

Even though the politics were against it, Menzies, McEwan and Casey, took the long view that trade with Japan was in Australia's interests. This was Australia's first step towards serious trade with Asia and was followed by similar agreements with Malaya in 1958 and 1959.

What also followed was an influx of foreign investment into Australia, not just from the United States but from Japan. It wasn't until 1 December 1960 that the Menzies government issued the first export licence for iron ore, overturning a 22-year ban. Japanese trading houses like Mitsui invested heavily in the development of Australia's mining and resources industry, setting Australia up to move from an export economy based largely on agriculture to one based on mining.

*Lessons from history*

What are the lessons from history as Australia charts this next chapter in our trade relations with Asia and the world? Australia's structural reforms of the 1980s and 1990s, coupled with the Howard government's concerted effort to sign free trade agreements through the early 2000s have created a strong set of liberal economic settings for Australia. Australia's 28 consecutive years of economic growth were the envy of the world, cut off only by the Covid-19 pandemic.

But the increasing strategic competition in the Indo-Pacific region and rising protectionism point to the end of easy trade wins in Asia. China and Russia's actions have led to major disruptions in global trade. We are seeing a bifurcation of the global economy based along ideological lines – the United

States, Europe and Australia have imposed sanctions on Russia, and restricted Chinese investment in telecommunications and critical infrastructure. Southeast Asia, Africa, and the Middle East take a more benign view. Coupled with the resurgence of protectionist voices in the United States, where depressed manufacturing communities have lost faith in free trade and the benefits of a globalised economy, the global rules-based liberal economic order is under huge pressure. As an open economy, Australia is at significant risk from the geoeconomic consequences of this shift.

China, a market which Australian exporters have relied upon heavily for the last three decades, has broken many of its economic ties with Australia over a few short years. Many industries were caught completely unprepared for the swift change in Australia's geopolitical environment – there were only so many lobsters Australians were willing to eat over their Christmas lunch, and ships laden with Australian coal floated off the coast of China for almost a year.

While some Australian exporters have managed to divert their exports to other markets, such as India, Japan, and South Korea, it has been more difficult to find new markets for exports like wine. Australia's wine exports to China declined in value by 97% in 2021, and overall wine exports by 30%.

Strategic competition hasn't just harmed Australia. It is also hurting those who seek to disrupt the status quo, namely China and Russia. Further, just because things are and will be difficult for China and Russia does not mean that their leadership will change course. For authoritarian regimes, the decision-making matrix does not mirror that of a democratic leader. Russia has strong economic ties with Britain and Europe, yet regardless of the economic consequences, it has started the first major war in Europe in 30 years with its invasion of Ukraine in February 2022. The Chinese Communist Party's (CCP) aim is to maintain control of the country; economic considerations and consequences are of secondary importance. The CCP's recent decisions illustrate the primacy of power, pride, and face over economics. For example, trade embargoes against Australian producers sought to 'teach' Australia a lesson, regardless of the local Chinese consumer's desire to drink Australian shiraz. Similarly, purporting to deal with Covid-19 through an elimination strategy allows the CCP to keep control (or at least be seen to keep control) of the policy narrative and the population despite causing China potentially to plunge into a recession for the first time since the 1920s. Finally, talk of taking back Taiwan is about restoring national pride, which trumps the potentially catastrophic impact on economic growth that a war might have.

For Australia, it is imperative to take a long view in the face of the current challenges. This does not mean that Australia should join in moves towards protectionism or give in to pressure from China. On the contrary, Australia's economy and history of trade liberalisation mean, in the absence of US leadership in this space, it is even more important that we advocate for open markets. This is particularly the case considering there is now bipartisan agreement in the United States against certain new free trade arrangements such as the Comprehensive and Progressive Agreement for Trans-Pacific Partnership. There is more need than ever for Australia to bring its creative diplomatic nous to the trade agenda, in particular when it comes to expanding the sphere of influence of liberal democracies among those whose preference is to hedge.

Menzies was a firm believer that trade between nations begets peace. In 1965, he remarked that "the greatest guarantee of peace in the world is that nations should trade peacefully, plentifully and profitably with each other. This is a tremendous foundation for understanding and therefore for peace".[6] Until recently, the Menzies view rang true. As the global economy became more integrated and interdependent, the prospect of war between close trading partners seemed like a distant prospect.

But Menzies was also a realist. He would recognise that while our globalised economy has created a web of interdependencies, rising strategic competition and great power rivalry means Australia can no longer hedge. It must make clear it is on the side of freedom, not authoritarianism. We need, however, to recognise the reality that the global economy is likely to become more and more bifurcated, Australia must look to diversify its markets, expanding not just who we export to but what we export. The recent signing of a trade agreement with the United Kingdom proves that what is old can be new again. The opportunities for Australia's energy exports to Europe, particularly clean energy, are huge, as are those for Australia's world-leading healthcare system. Australia also has a plethora of natural resources including precious metals, base metals, ferrous and non-ferrous metals, coal, oil, gas, hydrogen, and uranium. These resources have been, are and will remain

---

6    Menzies, R. 1965.

a core component of global demand in an industrialised age. Australia's developing relationship with India also presents another important opportunity for diversifying our export markets while working with like-minded liberal democracies. But this will require some degree of economic bravery, both from policymakers and exporters alike.

*Conclusion*

Menzies led a government from 1949 until 1966 that followed some of the Keynesian economic orthodoxies of the day, although he was careful to avoid government-funded pump priming of the economy. Despite significant opposition, Menzies and McEwen took decisions that responded to the geopolitical and economic conditions facing Australia. This required taking a long-range view of Australia's interests, putting aside short-term political gain and withstanding pressure to stick with the status quo.

Australia is the world's 13th-largest economy and has considerable diplomatic and strategic influence. We cannot take for granted the relative size of our economy nor the continuity of our strategic and trade relationships. We should seek to influence our strategic settings to ensure they are most favourable to our interests, but we must not be blind to the trends we face.

In the ensuing years, we need to learn the lessons from Menzies. Take the long view, be nimble when it comes to diversifying our markets, and build a community of like-minded nations through our diplomatic and economic influence. As Menzies showed us in the 1950s, it will be imperative to withstand pressure, both from within and outside. By taking the long view and putting the national interest ahead of short-term political gain, we can secure the future of Australia's economic prosperity and, most importantly, our freedom.

*Georgina Downer is the Executive Director of the Menzies Institute. She has previously been a diplomat and a lawyer.*

# 4

# Are markets anti-social?

## Craig Emerson

It's easy to view markets as being heartless, even anti-social, that they involve greedy people and unethical corporations and cannot possibly be an effective way of advancing the common good. Surely governments are best positioned to provide the services that contribute to social progress?

Markets are driven by self-interest so they can't do any good, right? Let's explore this idea by invoking the thoughts of the father of economics, Adam Smith. *In An Inquiry into the Nature and Causes of the Wealth of Nations* written almost 250 years ago, Smith observed:

> It is not from the benevolence of the butcher, the brewer, or the baker that we expect our dinner, but from their regard to their own self-interest.

Sounds greedy, doesn't it? But this was not Smith's accusation. Rather, he was observing a reality: that people engage in producing and trading goods and services to advance their self-interest. Yes, self-interest might include greed and unethical behaviour such as cheating each other in transactions, but it can also include people's desire to provide for their families or to earn money and give some of it to charity. It might even include a desire for a better world.

Self-interest is not the same as greed. Whatever constitutes self-interest, it is a powerful motivator. After all, whose interest are you serving if not your own?

Self-interested people come together as business owners and workers producing goods and services that customers desire and then exchanging them for money. They earn profits and wages in the process.

Acting in one's self-interest is not inherently bad behaviour. Nor are markets inherently bad. It's the nature of the activity that matters.

*Competition is good*

Smith has been viewed as someone who believes only in money and greed. In fact, Smith was a free marketer; he loathed cartels:

> People of the same trade seldom meet together, even for merriment and diversion, but the conversation ends in a conspiracy against the public, or in some contrivance to raise prices.

Collusive behaviour and the formation of cartels are indeed a conspiracy against the public. It's the main reason that governments enact competition laws prohibiting this sort of behaviour.

## A market for coffee

Consider a competitive market – producing and selling coffee. Café owners would like high prices for their coffee, but if one owner raises the price above the going price, customers will go elsewhere. And all the time, owners are working on how they might gain a competitive edge; finding better blends, attracting the best baristas, and renovating their café. Coffee drinkers would consider this a desirable market.

Suppose the government decided to supply coffee through state-run cafes or gave monopoly rights to a private corporation. Gone, or much diminished, would be the incentive to supply high-quality coffee at the lowest possible prices. And there would be little or no incentive to innovate; to try new blends and find ways to keep costs and prices low.

This is why in western countries, and even in most countries with socialist systems, the state does not run cafes or give monopoly rights to a private provider.

## Externalities

In lots of circumstances, the production and supply of goods and services can produce positive or negative externalities, or as they are called today, spillovers. A firm's research and development can produce valuable innovations. But since the originating firm cannot capture for itself all the benefits of its research and development, as others copy it either illegally or as patents expire, the firm will under-provide it from society's viewpoint. Research and development is therefore said to produce positive spillovers and a case can be made for the government to subsidise it.

This is especially the case for pure research, which might increase human understanding that eventually leads to valuable innovations. But firms will not tend to undertake pure research, because they will not be able to capture for themselves anywhere near the full commercial benefits of that research, which might not materialise for decades of further research and development.

Negative externalities, or negative spillovers, occur when an activity creates damage but is not charged a penalty for that damage. Too much of that good is produced from society's perspective. The penalty might take the form of an outright prohibition. For example, discharging water polluted with toxic chemicals into a waterway might be made illegal, or an international agreement to ban ozone-depleting chlorofluorocarbons put in place.

Alternatively, a price might be placed on the negative externality. A relevant example is putting a price on carbon emissions. The EU and a few other countries have placed a price on carbon through an emissions trading system. The Australian Government sought to place a price on carbon in 2009 but the legislation was defeated in the Senate. A price was placed on carbon in 2012 but was repealed by the new Australian Government in 2014.

In place of the carbon price, the Australian Government in 2014 began regulating the amount of carbon that could legally be released into the atmosphere by the larger emitters through what is called the Safeguard Mechanism.

*Are markets or regulations best to deal with negative spillovers?*

Going back to Smith, he marvelled at what he called the "invisible hand" of markets bringing buyers and sellers together and finding a price at which the market clears – where demand equals supply. This "invisible hand" is better at finding a price for coffee that consumers are willing to pay and at which producers are willing to supply coffee.

If governments regulated coffee production and sale, they wouldn't know the market-clearing price. If the government set the price each day, there would be a surplus of coffee on some days and a shortage on others.

Similarly, putting a price on a negative externality is likely to be far more effective than government officials trying to regulate it. If an overall limit is placed on the amount of carbon a country can emit into the atmosphere, then a market will form and work out the most efficient and effective way of complying with that limit. This is called a cap-and-trade system. A cap is placed on total emissions and businesses can trade in emissions permits, with those businesses that can reduce their emissions more easily selling their permits to businesses that find it harder to do so.

*A market for offsetting emissions*

Many nations have committed to zero *net* emissions by 2050 or earlier. Despite the best efforts of humankind, the world will be emitting carbon in 2050. Human and animal life on earth will emit carbon. So will forest fires from lightning strikes. Even if the world achieves zero net emissions by 2050, atmospheric concentrations of carbon dioxide will be at their highest levels in tens of thousands of years; we will only have succeeded in no longer making the situation worse.

That's why carbon offsets are so important and will increasingly be so. If humankind can store more carbon than we release, we will be making progress. The answer is to release less carbon and store more.

Australia, along with several other countries, has developed a market for carbon offsets. One Australian Carbon Credit Unit (ACCU) indicates that one tonne of carbon dioxide equivalent has been stored or avoided by a project.

ACCUs have been created under the Safeguard Mechanism established in 2014 for use by those emitters that exceed their permissible emission limits. In addition, ACCUs are purchased by businesses that are not covered by the Safeguard Mechanism but have nevertheless committed to reducing their emissions. During 2022, the price of ACCUs was broadly in the range of A$30-60.

The new Australian Government has committed to tightening the limits on permissible emissions for the big emitters covered by the Safeguard Mechanism. As these limits are tightened the value of ACCUs will tend to rise.

The Australian Clean Energy Regulator is in the process of establishing a properly functioning Carbon Exchange for trading in ACCUs. Other countries are establishing carbon exchanges too. These will bring together sellers and buyers of carbon credits. Under Article 6.2 of the Paris Agreement, countries that buy carbon credits of high integrity can count them towards their Nationally Determined Contributions to global emission reductions.

The Clean Energy Regulator intends that the Australian Carbon Exchange provides a premium on the price of ACCUs where the activity improves biological diversity in addition to offsetting carbon emissions. For example, revegetation of cleared land in biologically diverse regions would qualify for a premium.

A separate premium is envisaged where the activity achieves socially desirable goals. For example, early-season savanna burning by remote Indigenous communities reduces carbon emissions relative to those that would be emitted later in the dry season from lightning strikes when the savanna is fully grown. Income earned by these communities from ACCUs is being devoted to improving schools in remote communities, leading to higher attendance rates.

Of course, it is in the interests of the Clean Energy Regulator and in the national interest for carbon offsets to be of high integrity; that one ACCU truly represents one tonne of carbon dioxide equivalent stored or avoided. This maximises the price of ACCUs for those who generate them. The new Australian Government has announced a review of the integrity of ACCUs, which has since reported.

*Carbon markets for the common good*

Storing and avoiding carbon is for the common good. It is essential to achieving any goal of zero net emissions since the earth will be emitting carbon beyond 2050. Well-designed carbon markets are capable of identifying the best opportunities for storing and avoiding emissions and generating income for those engaged in these activities.

The alternative of government officials finding such opportunities and setting prices for carbon offsets would be as difficult as officials making coffee and setting a price for it or officials replacing Smith's butchers, brewers and bakers and producing these basic consumer goods. Carbon markets are a good example of harnessing the power of the market for the common good.

> *Craig Emerson is an economist who previously served as Minister for Small Business and Minister for Tertiary Education and Science in the Rudd and Gillard Governments.*

# 5

# The opportunity gap

## Jason Falinski

There is a tide in the affairs of men which, taken at the flood,
leads on to fortune; omitted, all the voyage of their life is bound in
shallows and in miseries.
(William Shakespeare, *Julius Caesar*)

Australia is in danger of unlearning the lessons of the past and
regressing into a slow-growth, high-inflation, low-opportunity
nation with declining living standards.

Before the global pandemic, Australia had spent several years
reversing economic reforms that ensured efficient and effective
allocation of scarce resources. It was almost like the successes
of previous generations allowed us to engage in harmful self-
indulgence. Rational arguments for reform and change, gave
way to irrational appeals to our emotions, demanding that
we care more about symbolic gestures rather than meaningful
outcomes.

The impact of this over a large gamut of policies damaged

our nation, our people and our institutions. Instead of the Australian economy expanding citizens' prospects, we have steadily reduced rungs on the ladder of opportunity. We have entrenched in legislation the power of vested interest.

Since 2007, there have been several major changes to public policy, all of which have had the impact of reducing productivity growth. The most problematic interventions have been in housing, finance, energy, industrial relations and education. A lack of will to reform Australia's fundamentally unfair and complex taxation system has resulted in opportunities being denied to current and future generations because our tax system incentivises destructive economic behaviour.

All these reversals and reform failures make Australia more vulnerable to external shocks. Australia is now going through a prolonged period of inflation, and the poor policy settings in each of these areas mean that the cost of adjustment is higher. These costs are only recognised long after they are paid, and the causes are too often apportioned to symptoms that have nothing to do with the situation. Resulting in corrective action that makes things even worse.

If we as a nation undertook fundamental reform it would be the spark that set off a renaissance. The reason productivity is so important is that it allows a society to provide a better life for its citizens. Martin Luther King said that the long arc of history bends towards justice. This is true because capitalism compels it to do so.

The human spirit demands the fundamentals of justice: equality, freedom and fairness. Economic productivity not only embodies these values but also enables them. Seen through this lens, economic reform is not just a financial issue or even a vote-winning tactic, it is a moral issue as old as the scriptures.

Australia's history with economic reform is not a glorious one. Our federation was cobbled together after the Left opposed it because they wanted to protect state-sponsored industry at a state level. It was only a 'dirty' deal between the Free Traders and the Protectionists, in which Protectionists agreed to free trade amongst the colonies while Free Traders agreed to protectionist policies outside those colonies.

From this point, it was mostly downhill. The Australian Settlement had three key pillars: the white Australia policy; protected industries behind a tariff wall; and centralised wage fixing. Each had long-term deleterious impacts on Australia and its people. The White Australia policy was racist, it is a stain on our national history. It further isolated Australia both in the region and the world. It also meant that the best and the brightest who wanted to contribute to our nation's future were prevented from doing so for no better reason than the arbitrary place in which they were born.

Once you accepted that discrimination based on race rather than merit as a founding principle other silly and destructive ideas become much easier. In this case, it was embedding the power of unions and industry groups through government-supported companies hiding behind a tariff wall. This then enabled the preposterous idea that a commission sitting in Melbourne could set not only pay rates but also work conditions for all companies right across the country. Both foundations were disenfranchising. In Australia, it became more important to have the right people in your back pocket rather than getting your product in the consumers' back pockets.

In such an environment corruption became rampant. Gerard Henderson highlighted not even the tip of the iceberg of this in his article *The IR Club*. The Hawke Government was forced to deregister the BLF, the forerunner of the CFMMEU.

When the ALP went to the next logical step of proposing the nationalisation of banks, something that some members of the National Party today are not opposed to, Australians responded negatively and elected the Menzies Government in 1949.

The Menzies Government was not a reformist government. It was a competent government. Changes were small and gradual. Having said that Robert Menzies, against the opposition of the Left, dismantled the White Australia policy, leading to Harold Holt's announcement that it had been abandoned in 1965. His government also undertook the great project of bringing Australians together, firstly by giving everyone a stake in the Australian economy through home ownership, then by seeking to dismantle anti-Catholic sentiment, and finally with the 1968 referendum that empowered the federal government to make laws for the benefit of Indigenous Australians.

Today, the Whitlam Government would be described as a hot mess, rather than the visionary crusaders that Left-wing historians paint them as. If you are in any doubt as to which characterisation is most accurate, please take the time to read the front pages of the Sydney Morning Herald from 1972 to 1975. It is hard to pick a favourite scandal from this time but certainly, the decision of a minister to raise funds privately through a middle-man using petrodollars so he could buy Australian mines is hard to top. You can imagine Rex Connor ringing his broker buying BHP shares on his private account which in due course he would transfer to the Treasury along with his privately arranged debt facility.

Gough Whitlam introduced economic programs that created a Keynesian debt trap and supercharged inflation. As his programs doubled inflation, he responded by doubling wages, which then doubled prices, leading to higher wage demands, and higher price increases, baking in inflationary expectations.

Such were the fruits of Left-wing economic programs. He lost in an absolute landslide after a controversial dismissal that should have set him up for a resounding victory.

If possible, history should judge the Fraser Government even more harshly. It knew better and still did not act. Fraser held a record number of cabinet meetings, to reach a record low number of meaningful decisions. Fraser thought the problem was managing the system when the system was not managing.

Australian policymakers resumed the historical trend, making the right decisions having exhausted all other options. Through the 1980s and 1990s, a series of economic reforms lead to important advancements for Australia and its citizens. By reforming product markets, it became possible to run the economy faster without triggering inflation. We were able to achieve this by deregulating Labor markets, capital markets, tax and welfare and federation reforms. Governments at the State and Federal levels were focused on outcomes for citizens rather than powerful sectorial interests.

These reforms opened Australia up to the world, created boundless opportunities and in turn, we became more globally integrated and more influential. We were key to significant agreements that made our nation, our region and our world safer, more prosperous and peaceful.

Australia avoided three major global downturns, our national income per capita rose in real terms by 73%, our current account moved from systemic deficit to surplus, and income inequality was reduced. Not to mention Australian diplomats were central to ending apartheid in South Africa, an Antarctic treaty and the formation of APEC, all while reducing our carbon emissions by 21%.

That all came to an end in 2007. The Rudd government was elected to do three fundamental things: sign the Kyoto Agreement, apologise to the Stolen Generation and rewind WorkChoices. Of course, Rudd did far more and far worse. He used the Global Financial Crisis to bake in permanent deficits, reallocated money from productive to unproductive sectors, and began reregulating the banking sector through legislation like the Responsible Lending Act and the Fair Work Act.

It never ceases to amaze that political commentators seem unable to follow the direct line between record-low real wage growth and the implementation of the Fair Work Act.

The Abbot, Turnbull and Morrison Governments at various points did try to undertake moderate reforms, but at every point were met with vehement opposition from entrenched interest groups without any counterbalance. Indeed the opposite happened, to get several issues off the table, legislation was introduced that made bad situations worse. The most egregious example would have to be the Gonski 2.0 reforms. From today's perspective, it makes the achievements of the Hawke Government even more admirable.

It is possible to take some hope too. We are almost certainly about to go through a period of elevated inflation. Inflation, unlike unemployment, hurts everyone, the vulnerable most. It is no coincidence that at the end of the 1970s, our last period of sustained inflation, the people of the United Kingdom and the United States elected two leaders who were considered dangerous right-wingers.

Ronald Reagan and Margaret Thatcher managed to get elected by promising to fix the underlying problems facing their nations. They were credible because they spoke to the moral imperative of their programs and the logical nature of them. Then, as now, the Left were morally suspect on a whole raft of issues including race, human rights and irrational outcomes of their supposed compassion.

If Australia is to return to a high growth, low inflation economy with opportunities for all, the program is pretty simple to outline, even though it will be difficult to implement.

It is time to admit that Gonski 2.0 is a failure. The billions that have been outlaid have made education outcomes for students and families worse. No one wants to say this because it activates the education unions and academics whose livelihoods rely on generous public sector subsidies without accountability.

What has emerged from overseas experimentation with education policy from Asia to North America and Western

Europe are some very clear principles: decentralised schools with maximum freedom to experiment with different methodologies; funding follows students so when families move their children from a failing school to a succeeding one, the failing school stops operating; teacher quality and curriculum matters far more than class size. And more technology does not lead to better outcomes.

Other elements are up for debate. In some countries later starts to formal schooling seems to have beneficial outcomes, in others earlier schooling seems to have some benefits. Experts now agree that physical activity has a material impact on social development and academic success.

One thing for which there is no evidence is more funding equates to better outcomes.

In Australia, we have done the opposite, not just failed to do this, but done the opposite over the last two decades.

The cost of continuing with this policy is that eventually millions of Australians will find it more difficult to find fulfilling work in an increasingly globalised labour market. This is the simple choice facing leaders in Australia today: do they continue to acquiesce to an establishment whose interests are primarily its own, or support the disempowered students and families who are just looking for a better future?

Australia's housing market has a claim to be our worst policy failure since federation. As a nation we have everything going for us: we have plentiful land, cheap materials and relatively efficient capital markets enabling borrowing for housing. And yet home ownership has been falling because we have failed to build enough houses.

The impact of this is fewer people own a stake in the future of our nation and are less incentivised to preserve and promote its success. Further, and more seriously, the fall in home ownership is the biggest cause of wealth inequality in our nation, indeed globally.

Listening to the experts explain the reasons for our housing crisis is hilarious. A more talented writer, say, Dave Chappelle, could turn it into a five-hour skit. People who are responsible for the education of the next generation of housing planners intone seriously that increasing the supply of housing increases prices. This is the equivalent of a physicist doubting the existence of gravity and arguing for it to be ignored.

The very same people who argue strenuously that we need to increase the supply of 'social' housing (which is the Left's rebranding of public housing) will then in the next paragraph vote against increasing the supply of private housing. The over-regulation of housing by the same people who decry its cost is hypocritical. The case for increasing supply is clear, it is morally right, and its denial is a betrayal of younger generations.

If we cannot undertake reform of these two critical areas which have outsized impacts on the prosperity of our nation what chance do we have of undertaking significant and critical renovation of our tax and welfare system including our superannuation system? At the moment, our tax system is a black box in which governments ask the ATO to collect as much money as possible to fund programs that do very little good. The ATO has asked for and received extraordinary powers that deny Australian citizens basic rights.

If many government programs were subjected to the rigours of private sector analysis their lack of delivery would see many discarded. Indeed, many do more harm than good much less enough good to justify their ongoing funding.

Our tax system is complex, uncertain, counterproductive, difficult to comprehend, inefficient and unfair. It has been designed to raise money, not operate as part of an entrepreneurial and fair nation. The tax system punishes reward and discourages risk.

Instead, its complexity incentivises economic activity for the pure purpose of optimising a tax outcome rather than providing a needed service or product. In other words, our tax system incentivises companies to only innovate with their accountants rather than their research and development department.

Many bemoan the fact that we do not have enough world-class companies. The tax system is largely the explanation for that. Those global companies when you look beneath the hood have a healthy capability set in tax optimisation structures which they then deploy in other parts of the world. Australia leads the world in tax planning and funding of class action lawsuits.

This is how our human capital ends up being misallocated and wasted. In most other nations the best and the brightest go to work for entrepreneurs like Elon Musk putting spaceships on Mars, or electric cars through tunnels created by the state-of-the-art boring machines that are making tracks for a hyperloop controlled by someone's brain through a neural link.

Who knows maybe in the future our best and brightest will be able to use devices from neural link to interface directly with our tax system.

It may come to pass that Australia's tax system saves humanity. If ever an evil AI becomes conscious and gets loose, humanity will be able to buy enough time to get all of us off the planet by throwing the Income Tax Assessment Act and enabling legislation at it. That is one maze it ain't finding its way out of any time soon.

There is a myriad of other areas just screaming out for reform, especially in industrial relations, energy, health, transport and infrastructure. Better alignment of expenditure and revenue would be a first step, so instead of States doing the spending while the federal government does the taxing, there is alignment. States run away from this idea like Dracula from a sunrise.

Put together this would allow our community to more efficiently and effectively allocate scarce resources where it can do its best for all Australians, indeed for everyone on this planet. Each reform suggested above empowers individuals, encourages them to take responsibility and ensures public servants are more accountable. It is the ultimate program of equality and fairness.

More important than all of that is that it provides more opportunities for people to live the best lives of their choosing. This should be the key objective of every government, in every part of the world: to maximise the freedom of the individual wholly consistent with others, so that they can live the best lives of their choosing. As John the Savage at the end of a *Brave*

*New World* would have it free to succeed and free to fail, we would have all of it.

Those who so often claim the mantle of justice are the very ones most active in opposing the reforms that enable its emergence. It is long overdue that this was made clear.

*Jason Falinski is the chair of Airtrip. He was the Member for Mackellar between 2016 and 2022.*

# 6

# Government by the people
# Gigi Foster and Paul Frijters

The Australian political system is well-known to be highly corrupt, a problem exacerbated by the covid-era policy failures. Where could a reform movement start? We argue that the state bureaucracy, currently highly politicised and intertwined with external special interests via revolving doors and other 'Games of Mates', can be re-harnessed to the goal of advancing the public interest by creating a parallel democratic structure to augment our present electoral and political institutions. The task of this new structure would be to appoint the top level of the government bureaucracy and other state-aligned organisations through the use of decision-making citizen juries. We also offer a second proposal that aims to democratise media production itself. Our proposals aim to create both a more independent media sector and a more pro-social public sector capable of withstanding the temptations created by high inequality and deep corruption within the political class. We sketch our proposals and show how they unite the positive elements of competition, nationalism, and independence to craft a more democratic and robust foundation on which to build Australia's future.

*Introduction*

In this chapter, we take it as proven that both major political parties in Australia are thoroughly corrupt in the sense that they serve their own and minority interests, rather than the public interest. This corruption is not in plain sight, as that would be too easy for the public to discover, but most frequently takes the form of favour exchange between politicians and businessmen quietly working together over time for their mutual benefit and to the impoverishment of the man on the street. Writing of this *Game of Mates* played by politicians and others (whom they call James) using their power to advance themselves at the expense of everyday Australians, Cameron Murray and Paul Frijters (2022) write:

> Cases of individual theft and fraud are relatively easy to discover. It would be far too easy to combat this behaviour from a few 'bad eggs', who can be removed from their position of power. Such behaviour can easily be identified as corruption and be punished as such.
>
> But with a group of loyal Mates who also involve themselves in making the rules and exercising discretion over who gets the grey gifts they control, James is able to conduct the Game with ease and out of sight. James need not favour himself directly. Rather, James favours his Mates, who later return the favour to him and others in their 'club'. Together, James and his Mates create an informal group by trading direct or indirect reciprocal favours, which over time evolves into a social structure that bears a remarkable resemblance to a mafia.

We take it as given that this corruption in the political sphere has seeped into the top of the public sector, the major corporations, and the media. These institutions are all now oriented towards worsening inequality via monopolisation of their respective 'markets' and in other ways ensuring the absence of true competition, thereby impoverishing and enslaving the vast majority of the Australian people. What we now observe in Australia is a mix of fascism (i.e., a power-obsessed elite presiding over a merger of state and corporate bodies) and feudalism (i.e., the mental and physical domination of the majority by a small minority).

In this chapter, we take seriously the question of what types of reforms could work to put the public interest back into contention within Australia's powerful institutions. Our answer to this question starts by recognising that the problem is sufficiently large and complex that the only feasible solutions are either revolution, which we hope Australia can avoid, or a carefully designed adjustment to a vulnerable, crucial, and manipulable element in the present system. As such an element, our first proposal targets the top layer of the public sector, taking the optimistic view that Australia's public sector leadership cadre can be rescued and made to return to a pro-social orientation. In our second proposal, we discuss how the information commons can be democratised.

The reform ideas we discuss in this chapter centre on the concept of citizen juries, which are public-service organisations that can be used to break the link between party politics and bureaucratic decisions. We make the case for how our ideas would increase the representation of market forces and factors in our system of governance and conclude by discussing other benefits that we foresee.

*Beyond saving? The corruption in Australian politics and bureaucracy*

In what ways have Australian institutions been hijacked to serve special interests, and in what ways is the country still a democracy?

Australia is still a democracy in the sense that there is compulsory voting and new political parties can compete in elections. Elections matter, since significant power is concentrated in the hands of the majority in Commonwealth and State Parliaments. New parties must fight to grow in an extremely hostile and politically biased climate, facing uphill battles such as the public funding of established parties that serves as a barrier to entry for others, but still, new parties can compete. Anti-democratic hurdles simply mean that democratic renewal is far more difficult than it is supposed to be, a point illustrated by the recent failure of the growing number of 'freedom-friendly minor parties,' promoting the restoration of freedom after two years of the most destructive peacetime policy-making in Australia's history, to win a single seat in the May 2022 Australian federal elections.[7] Still, renewal is not impossible, particularly not in local politics where opposition groups can more easily organise.

In what ways is Australia shown to have a thoroughly corrupted political and economic class? In the ways detailed in Murray and Frijters' 2017 book about Australian corruption, *Game of Mates*: a very small minority is now used to doing favours for each other across public and private boundaries, in terms of favourable legislation, revolving doors, dismantled anti-corruption bodies, elite-compliant courts, party-aligned media whose

---

7   McLellan, S, "Chasing 'freedom' at the Federal Election", *The Spectator*, 2002.

business model is to sell access to the public, careerist political parties that internally reward loyalty to special interests, and systems of education and cultural production controlled and directed towards the interests of the elite minority. During the covid period we observed a further strengthening of the vast network of grey gifts between the government and big business that were already strongly in operation before covid, a phenomenon also evident overseas, as discussed further in our 2021 book, *The Great Covid Panic*.

As noted in *Game of Mates* and its 2022 sequel, *Rigged* – which includes an analysis of the covid period – the endemic corruption of the main political parties involves an alliance with large corporations whose prime target in their involvement in politics is to ensure the absence of true competition. Crises, including but not limited to the covid crisis, are exploited by this alliance to further monopolisation and increase barriers to entry. An example is provided by the 2007-2009 Great Financial Crisis, in which the big Australian banks scored against the competing foreign and loan banks that had been making inroads into the mortgage market business. This win resulted from preferential guarantees handed out by the government to the big banks.[8] How this unfolded was that in the financial panic of late 2008, the government first announced a blanket guarantee of domestic bank accounts, with perhaps some costs for accounts over AU$1 million. While it later announced that foreign banks and mortgage loan banks would also get access to the government guarantee, the damage had already been done, as investors had already pulled out of those banks. The

---

8    Smith, A, "The Australian Government Guarantee Scheme for Large Deposits and Wholesale Funding (Australia GFC)", *Journal of Financial Crises*, 2020.

nature of the game in this instance was that politicians facing the GFC crisis rushed to look after those in their club – i.e., their mates at the big banks – and then later made a cosmetic adjustment to make their decision look less unfair than it was. As another prime example in the realm of finance, the Australian superannuation industry in general is largely made up of mandated monopolies and preferential rules embedded into opaque regulations and contracts.[9]

The grim reality is that neither of the two political parties is better than the other. A major capitulation towards foreign-owned special interests happened on the watch of Labor in 2010 when Julia Gillard agreed to legislation that benefited several hundred mining companies that had been the target of the previous PM's super-profits tax proposal, created a tax scheme that yielded only meagre revenues and bound the Commonwealth government to prevent the taxation of mining companies by state governments.[10] The superannuation scam, in which high yearly overheads enrich a small cabal of union directors and employers at the expense of workers, was Labor legislation and has been continuously championed for expansion by former Labor Prime Minister Paul Keating.[11] The Liberals, for their part, have given out billions during the covid years to companies that did not need it,[12] subsidised elite-renewing private schools,[13] ignored the findings of

---

9    Drew, M, and Stanford, J, "A Review of Australia's Compulsory Superannuation Scheme After A Decade", *Queensland University of Technology Discussion Paper*, 2003.
10   "Australia's Gillard cuts deal with mining companies on taxes", *CNN*, 2010.
11   Kohler, A, "Paul Keating says Australians owed superannuation increase after being 'robbed' of real wage adjustments', *ABC*, 2021.
12   Cockburn, G, "Treasury concedes JobKeeper paid billions to profit-making businesses", *The Canberra Times*, 2021.
13   Chrysanthos, N, "NSW private schools reaped $72 million in JobKeeper payments", *The Sydney Morning Herald*, 2022.

bank misbehaviour by the Hayne Commission,[14] organised several public-private partnership deals that disregarded the public interest and bypassed the checks and balances of the Departments of Transport (as documented in Murray and Frijters 2022), and so on. We regard it as self-evident that the Australian political and economic system today blends fascism and feudalism and grows like a fungus on the increasingly hollowed-out tree of formerly democratic institutions.

While it may seem inevitable that Australia's bid for democracy will end in a coup by political and economic elites that reverses the country rapidly into formalised fascist tyranny, we still see the possibility of renewal. Our hopes are founded on several observations.

First, the damage done at the behest of Australia's elites to the health and productive base of the country during the covid era makes the country as a whole weaker, and this is not in the interests of the military or other pro-Australia forces, including patriotic citizens. Second, large companies, state governments, and other factions are each other's rivals just as often as they find it in their interests to collaborate, making it very unlikely that all or even a majority of such forces can agree on and effectively implement a coup. Third, Australia's local populations remain relatively cohesive – our local communities have not been destroyed – and they are accustomed to having some say in local politics. Finally, the inherent mismanagement and impoverishment endemic to a more autocratic and monocultural system naturally engenders

---

14    Butler, B, "Banking royal commission: most recommendations have been abandoned or delayed", *The Guardian*, 2021.

a countermovement. The central question in our view is thus when (not whether) there will be a reform movement strong enough to overcome the incumbent loose coalitions of corrupt actors. As freethinking intellectuals, we see it as our role to provide blueprints for what to aim for in such a reform movement.

### Citizen juries as an alternative

One core systemic barrier to Australian institutions' ability to serve the public is that both politicians and outside wealthy interests can corrupt the public sector. Elected politicians can politicise the top of the public sector by simply appointing corporate interests as heads of particular public-sector roles, for example. For their part, corporate interests can infiltrate the public sector by offering lucrative careers to top public servants or their families. Both such means of anti-competitive public-sector capture by elites are now entirely normal, and the second is itself enough to ensure that concentrated wealth will corrupt the public sector even if politics were to be completely 'cleaned up'.

How then can the leaders of the public sector be brought back on the side of the public, and in a way that makes it hard for political and economic elites to re-capture? What institutions could be established to manage the appointments of people to roles at the top of the public sector that skirt the power of elected politicians or special interests – institutions that will further have some regard for their own longevity, without becoming a major problem of their own?

What we suggest in answer to this question is a new sortition-based democratic arm of government that can be sewn onto the body of Australian politics. The core job of this new arm would be to appoint the entire top layer of the public sector and of any organisations that are strongly financially dependent on the state or that have a public orientation. The subgroup of citizens making any given appointment decision would be a citizen jury. The outcome of the deliberation of each citizen jury would be to fill one role, with potentially dozens or even hundreds of juries operating simultaneously each year as the operationalisation of this new arm of government. An existing institution that could be charged with establishing and becoming the organising hub of these citizen juries is the current set of Electoral Commissions. These bodies have the infrastructure required – lists of citizens and volunteers around the country – to be able ideologically and practically to own and implement the citizen jury system.

Imagine that our proposal became reality and that 10 years from now in Australia, there is a citizen-jury system for appointments to the entire upper layer of the public sector. Politicians would still be in charge of policy and budgets, but juries would appoint all the top people working in the public sector. The system would apply to all large entities receiving significant state funding, meaning all of the following and more: universities, large hospitals, government departments, state media, arts councils, statistical agencies, and the judiciary.

We sketch below what the operation of a citizen jury would look like for, say, appointing the director of the Australian Broadcasting Corporation.

20 random adult citizens are selected from the household register. These 20 are given a budget and a time frame to appoint a new director of the ABC, who would be appointed for 5 years. This is a civic duty for which they are compensated and get time off work. They meet in person, just like juries in criminal cases.

No 'minders' tell the jury how to do their job. The jury composition is kept secret until the decision is handed down. The jury's sole task is to come up with a name, a brief justification for why they have chosen the appointed candidate, and an explanation of expenses made. There is no set of requirements handed to the jury by existing politicians or bureaucrats, with the only input to their deliberations being a simple description of the set of tasks required of the person to be appointed to the role. The jury makes its procedures, finds its outside advice, and decides for itself what matters. Its members deliberate on such questions as 'what do we expect from a state broadcaster?' 'What kind of person could do this?' 'Where should we look for suitable candidates?' and 'How are we going to decide?'

These juries would have basic administrative support such as email, a website, accommodation, and so on. A specific institution like the Electoral Commission, run by people themselves appointed by citizen jury, would organise the juries and would look for improvements and champion the system.

Once erected, this citizen jury system could quickly take over all appointments to the top layer of the public sector, and within a short period, it could succeed in replacing the incumbent corrupted elite with people selected by a jury (noting that incumbents could apply for consideration). The jury system would also be responsible for appointing stand-bys in case a nominated person is ill, jailed, or refuses a job offer. Alumni of this system – i.e., former jury members who developed particular expertise in deliberation and how to efficiently sift through candidates – would be available to assist new juries if needed.

The intended benefits of this system are both short-term and long-term. The immediate short-term benefit is that the influence upon internal public-sector resource allocation of existing politicians and large wealth is broken. The reliance on the general public to make leadership decisions should also be expected to result in the appointment of leaders who are more pro-public than the present crop of Australian leaders because both their current job and their likely future jobs (i.e., other top positions within the public sector) would depend on the choices of random juries made up of that public.

The intended longer-term benefits of the citizen jury system flow partly via a more activated and constantly engaged citizenry that is taken seriously. The system promotes a more informed and self-aware citizenry that would in turn serve as more of a bulwark than today's Australian citizenry against future corruption and autocracy. Furthermore, the diversity of the population would more fully and automatically be reflected in the many leaders appointed, which would increase the number of viewpoints within the public sector, thus increasing its collective intelligence.

Another intended long-term benefit is the counterbalance to politicians provided by a layer of leaders in the public sector who have an independent democratic mandate. These leaders should be expected to keep to the law and hold politicians to account much more than is presently done. Also, as a group, those appointed by juries would develop immense expertise about how Australia's web of regulations and laws benefit insiders and special interests. This knowledge would help them to dismantle those unfair benefits. What is today impossible for any small group to understand and undo should be possible for this whole layer as a collective.

Would it be better to have a referendum-based system? The problem with referenda is that they do not beget public-oriented decision-makers, so while the voice of citizens may be heard on one particular issue, the underlying corrupting mechanisms remain in place, hidden under the seemingly democratic institution of referenda. Also, modern state bureaucracies are incredibly complex, with regulations that run into hundreds of thousands of pages. Referenda are not set up for ensuring the public interest is maintained in that kind of complex environment. Better, we argue, to appoint insiders who are public-oriented to oversee and direct that web of regulations as their main job, rather than to ask the public to make a handful of referenda decisions that will translate only poorly into complex regulation that truly serves the public.

Another natural response to Australia's predicament would be to call for massive wealth redistribution and the jailing of former elites, making this the object of a reform movement. One reason not to prefer this option is that aiming for such an outcome might engender civil war and massive capital flight. Another is that one probably needs to retain some of the current elites to have a successful reform movement, in which case the main reforms must address the longer-term problems without immediately threatening all vested interests.

## The media question

There is a second reform imperative: namely, how to produce a pro-public media sector. The core task of the fourth estate as the guardians against political hubris and abuse of power has not been achieved in recent decades, across the Western world. A deep reason for this failure is that the internet has undermined the advertising-based revenue model the media used to have, with many top media companies being unable to pay for high-quality investigative reporting, and therefore opting instead to employ lower-paid journalists who are happy to parrot whatever interest-group-aligned think tanks send to them. Connected to this problem is that vested interests can buy direct access to the public from media conglomerates. Keeping unfavourable stories out of the public gaze, and running negative stories on opponents, have become valuable commodities for which there are now implicit markets of NGOs and professional influencer firms.[15]

Part of this market operates inside the large multi-sector conglomerates that now run media empires, with Rupert Murdoch's empire a good case in point. Murdoch makes a loss on newspapers and news-oriented TV channels, while making a large profit on commercial sports channels, merely using the 'news' arm of the business to put pressure on governments to

---

15    Fuller, R, "The billionaire takeover of civil society", *Spiked,* 2021.

give his company special deals. This is an example of how the media have become in essence an extortion racket, reflecting the economic reality that the ability to influence public opinion now has far more commercial value than the ability to rake in advertising.

What is to be done? A successful reform effort must first recognise that the media landscape, not physical battlefields, is the place where modern warfare occurs. The wars of the 21$^{st}$ century are and will continue to be largely media wars, pitting countries, corporations, ideologies, regions, cities, and reform movements against each other. Social media has in recent years weaponised social networks in which people trust each other. The business model of a large social media company is to hijack interpersonal trust, turning it into a weapon when some selected viewpoint is made to seem socially dominant through the quiet censorship of unwanted opinions expressed between people. When he is made to think that people only share certain opinions amongst their peers, the social media user is given the impression that those opinions – the 'acceptable' ones, from the point of view of the media company – are the new social norm. Through this subtle but powerful means of control, large social media companies have hacked into the social consciousness of populations and the inherent deep need of humans to want to follow what is acceptable in their perceived group.

Working forward from the realities that the media have become a forum for mass warfare, that populations are currently abused by the media, and that any profit-oriented media company will sell its ability to influence opinions to the highest bidder, the logical solution is some kind of population-wide competitive production of media. By this, we do not mean national media, though national media with leaders appointed via citizen jury is not a bad place to start, but more broadly a system built by and of a population regularly engaged in the direct production and sifting through of news and information. If media is the new arena in which wars are waged, then the population must arm itself and be involved in those wars. In short, we would need a kind of national media conscription army, with the population trained in media combat, and in which the army draws on the population's combined knowledge, mobilising this powerful force for the benefit of the whole.

What could this look like? Many options can be created for different countries and cultures, bearing in mind a few key principles. First, one should not want or expect to generate a single truth or a single opinion for the country as a whole. On the contrary, as one might judge the health of a marketplace by the availability of alternative products, a measure of the success of a new media system would be the perennial airing of many different perspectives so that the population as a whole has the opportunity to be exposed to and reflect on this diversity. In a healthy system, each set of opinions is well-grounded, well-articulated, and produced well, drawing on the knowledge and skills of those involved in constructing it. This could be accomplished by implementing a short period of national training in media and media manipulation techniques, much like physical conscription armies are trained in the use of weapons, followed by one or more periods of 'active media duty' as part of one of many smaller media units. The units could be state-specific, religion-specific, sector-specific, ideology-specific, or in any other way 'group'-specific. Their identities and articulated positions should be expected to reflect the views of the existing population, developing as those views change. One way to facilitate the organic emergence of these groups is to apply the same principle as is used with calling referenda in Switzerland: to build from the signatures and time commitments collected from registered voters.

A second principle is to avoid pressing everyone into a similar role. As in any production process or marketplace, different individuals have different sets of knowledge and are best used in different ways. One person might best spend her months of media duty writing articles about chess competitions, while someone else would be best placed formulating quality signals that are placed on all articles and research projects about, say, Latin America. One might best produce funny fly-fishing videos and another in-depth reporting on problems with chemical plants. At a fundamental conceptual level, the aim is to release a kind of market mechanism to direct people to their most useful role inside these media institutions, which requires the formation of price signals and some notion of both preferences and externalities. Just how to set this up best is not a trivial exercise, and can involve combinations of market thinking and novel democratic designs. We leave the design specifics, the inevitable trial and error, and the ultimate reward of helping change the country into a less corrupt and more truly democratic place to others and our future selves.

*Conclusion*

Australia today is beleaguered with endemic political corruption and has been weakened economically, socially, psychologically, and physically after 3 years of abuse at the hands of corrupt elites, only the latest and most tragic bookend to decades of receding democracy. We propose a restorative reformation program that draws on the power of the people to break the corrosive connection between political and economic power, on the one hand, and direct control over both resource allocation and information flows, on the other. Our proposals for citizen juries and a program of citizen media service are intended to democratise core institutions such as the bureaucracy and the media, liberating them from the elites who have kidnapped them, and thereby raising the voice of the people in making key decisions and unleashing the power of diversity and competition between 'truths' in news production. By targeting more competition, the independence of institutions from money, and the creation of a useful form of national service through which to channel people's love for their country, Australia can 'build back better'.

About the authors: Gigi Foster is a Professor with the School of Economics at the University of New South Wales. Paul Frijters is a prominent research economist and has published over 150 papers in fields including unemployment policy, discrimination and economic development.

# 7

# What are you doing with my money? If you can't tell me, you don't deserve to have it

## Robert Holt

Having spent over 25 years in Management Consulting, Private Equity and Investment Management, I have always felt the acute gravity of reciprocating the trust that clients and investors have placed in me. When people pay or invest money, they deserve a return. At the very least, they expect you to do your best to do what you said you would do and report on strategies and outcomes so they can decide whether they should persist in letting you take or keep their money.

In contrast, when I was a boy and my parents gave me pocket money, I didn't think about what return they were looking for. There was no expectation other than an expression of love, societal norms, and the development of my sense of independence. There were unspoken expectations. They didn't expect me to throw the money away or spend it illegally or immorally. That would have been a breach of trust. But beyond that, I was free to spend the money as I pleased.

I'd argue that paying tax belongs in the category of investment rather than pocket money. And while we can decide to vote a government in or out, imagine a fund manager that took your money and then remained silent on the strategies and outcomes of your investment. However, too often, that is what paying taxes feels like.

Three experiences have shaped my strong belief that it would greatly assist both government and the voting public to develop a mechanism to better measure and report the application of public funds. Specifically, how can we measure the return on taxpayer funds invested? These stories are as follows:

I once worked on a budget review project for a government department that provided a monopoly service with 100% penetration. Their marketing budget for this service was larger than a big four bank and four times larger than a national airline. When I asked why so much I was told this was the budget upon service launch, and if they didn't spend it they would lose this budget and they never knew when it might be needed. As a taxpayer, I remain unhappy with this reasoning.

Over lunch, a sitting MP reflected that he had completed a Master of Public Administration degree at one of the most prestigious universities in the country and Return on Investment was not a topic covered in the course. As a citizen, I am concerned by this.

I once delivered a supplier-efficiency program for a government department where our team achieved an annualised repeatable year-on-year procurement benefit of $30m for a one-off fee of $3m. I reflected to the client that it was enormously satisfying to deliver a net benefit to the taxpayer of $27m. The client looked at me alarmed and said with some assertion that this was a benefit for the Department, NOT the taxpayer. As a citizen, I am confused and dissatisfied with this response.

*Please. Do it for Sam and Daisy!*

Imagine this scenario. Sam inherits $100,000 from a kind Aunt and he asks Jo, a colleague at work to introduce him to anyone who can help him invest this money. Jo sets up a meeting with two friends who operate separately as independent financial advisors, Anna and Tim, whom she knows from university. The next day they meet at their office. Anna arrives wearing a professionally tailored business suit, accompanied by her long-standing friend Tim, who is more casually dressed in a grey cardigan and well-worn faded jeans. They each represent financial management companies. After some friendly banter and a recital of their qualifications, they each ask Sam to invest some of his money. What is the minimum information Sam would need to help him decide?

At a minimum, it would be logical to ask:

1. What will they invest the money in?
2. What would be the expected benefits of making such an investment?
3. How do they expect to achieve these benefits?
4. What are the risks and consequences?
5. What is the track record of this investment as a validation of their pitch?
6. Why is it in Sam's interests to invest?

Anna tells Sam that money makes money, and to combat inflation and grow your wealth, she thinks Sam should invest in joining a syndicate to enter a horse race. There are two horses in the race. It costs a million dollars to enter the race and the prize money is $100,000. One horse is a Shetland pony, and the other owned by her company is a thoroughbred from a long line of winners of prestigious races. They have raced once a year for the past 5 years, and the thoroughbred has never lost, normally finishing the race before the Shetland pony has reached halfway. For every $1 Sam invests and the thoroughbred wins, her company will pay him 10c at the end of the race and return Sam's capital of $1. In the unlikely event the thoroughbred loses, Sam loses his entire investment.

Tim says suggests that while financial returns are great, we all have a responsibility to make the world a better place. He shares he is a devoted Christian and quotes Galatians 6:2 "Bear ye one another's burdens, and so fulfil the law of Christ". He points out Sam seems like a good person and wants him to invest in his company's faith-based pension fund that has returned an average of 5% per annum for the past 10 years. The fund invests in listed equities of the world's most benevolent companies. It distributes the first 5% of profit to investors and re-invests all profits above 5% to charitable causes run by the fund. Over 10 years the charitable re-investment has been between 1% and 7% of the fund value and has always achieved the 5% distribution to investors. In the event the fund does not achieve 5%, any shortfall is carried forward until the fund achieves the 5% per annum average. He invites Sam to visit some of the previously homeless people the fund has housed, some sick people they provide care for, and disadvantaged people they educate to see the genuine difference the fund makes. He claims the fund is growing and every year they invest in more social programs, so investors' impact is always increasing, whilst earning Sam 5% per annum on his capital.

That evening at home while sharing dinner with his spouse, Daisy. Sam decides to invest the entire amount split between both opportunities, but they both have different views on how much to apportion to each. Both investments have very different objectives. Anna's opportunity offers up to $10,000 in financial return on investment with very little apparent risk, although there appears to be no real return to society. Tim's proposal offers half the financial return but has a very compelling social return that could change the lives of people in genuine need. They decide to make a chart based on the minimum information for a decision. It looks as follows:

| Question | Anna's proposal | Tim's proposal |
|---|---|---|
| What will they invest the money in? | Entering a horse race | Listed equities of benevolent companies |
| What would be the expected benefits of making such an investment? | 10% Return on investment | 5% Return on investment plus re-investment in social causes |
| How do they expect to achieve these benefits? | Prize money distribution | Earnings distributions and charity work |
| What are the risks and consequences? | Horse loses and capital gone | Lower or no distribution in one year made up for in future years |
| What is the track record of this investment as a validation of their pitch? | Paid out for last 5 years | Delivered 5% return for 10 years and improved charitable outcomes year-on-year |
| Why is it in Sam's interests to invest? | Makes the highest financial return | Delivers the greatest good to society |

Figure 1: Anna's and Tim's options

Having reviewed this table, Sam and Daisy decide to split the investment between the two opportunities 50/50 and review their portfolio mix at the end of the year.

In the background, the TV is covering the forthcoming State election. A well-known and experienced politician named Beau wearing a navy suit and red and blue striped tie seeking re-election announces a new policy to increase spending on education by 7.5%. Beau points out this increase is 2.5% higher than the opposition's policy, and that his Party cares more about education. The program then cuts to the opposition spokesman, Naomi, in a Fuchsia-coloured dress standing outside parliament house, who denounces the policy saying that only last week her party announced the breakthrough policy of 5%, and Beau was just trying to one-up her policy. As her policy was announced first, it is her party that deserves recognition for caring more about education, and Beau is being irresponsible in spending funds that the budget cannot afford.

Sam and Daisy discuss this policy issue, and how their investment decision framework might apply to this proposal. Sam points out that as a taxpayer, he is unsure what he is investing in, other than the fact that Naomi wants to spend more money on education, and Beau wants to spend even more than Naomi. Daisy agrees and says that voters don't have the sufficient attention span to listen to the policy detail, but it seems overly simplistic and even dangerous to conclude that because Beau wants to spend more than Naomi, he cares the most about education. Both Beau and Naomi are offering to invest more public funds in education, but for what return?

Sam thinks that the numbers have become meaningless, and the budget has not been in surplus for over a decade, so politicians make promises to spend public funds without reference to outcomes, and then in the future, they pick and choose which outcomes to highlight to demonstrate their Party's success or point out the opposition Party's failures.

As taxpayers, both Sam and Daisy both feel their contribution is unappreciated and the choice between Naomi's policy and Beau's policy does not respect the large amount of money they contribute in taxes to the government each year. "If only there was a way to hold politicians to account" Daisy cries in frustration. "You should run for office, Daisy!" Exclaims Sam. Your slogan could be "Only a government that delivers more for less can be trusted with your money".

*So what?*

This simple story highlights many challenges with our current system. I count the following, but I am sure you can come up with a few more:

- We have more transparency and empowerment when we make investment decisions with our own money than governments do with public funds
- The public feels disconnected from the quantum of funds being spent by the government
- There is no consistent measuring stick to compare government outcomes against public funds spent
- Without such a measurement, governments are not sufficiently recognised, incentivised or rewarded for efficiently creating value that optimizes cost and benefits.

*What is the solution?*

Developing a quantitative, unambiguous, and meaningful scorecard for key government services such as Education, Transport, Healthcare, Law and Order and Infrastructure that measures Return on Taxpayer Investment is complex but not impossible.

If we consider the following example where the major indicators of success (i.e. returns on investment) in school education are:

1. Retention: The percentage of school children remaining in high school
2. Attainment: The percentage of students achieving a high-school graduation certificate by the age of 19
3. Naplan performance: The percentage of students achieving a top-three band score (one above the state minimum standard) for years three, five, seven and nine
4. User satisfaction: Parent and student ratings of the quality of education and the resources provided

The taxpayer investment we measure these returns against are:

1. Funds paid by the state government
2. Funds paid by the federal government

Our model applied to Victorian Schools would look something like this:

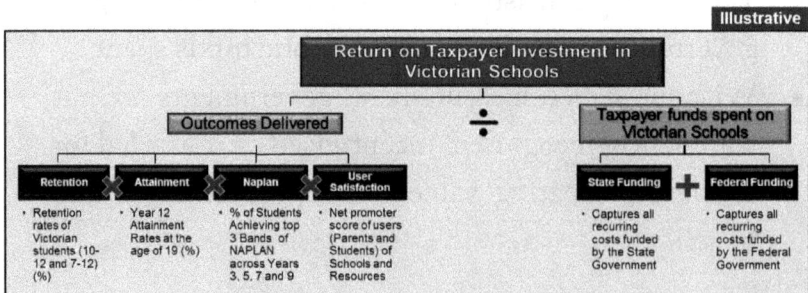

Figure 2: Victorian public school KPIs

Just like Sam and Daisy's investment, a one-year result is far more meaningful and informative when we can compare performance over multiple years. Many investment cases take time to yield results, and only by comparing results over an extended period can we truly gauge relative performance. Below is how we might apply this measure over successive years:

| Victorian Schools | 2015 | 2016 | Change | % Change |
|---|---|---|---|---|
| 10-12 Retention Rates | 84.8% | 85.0% | | |
| 7-12 retention Rates | 86.4% | 87.9% | | |
| Year 12 Attainment Rates | 89.5% | 92.6% | | |
| % of Students Achieving top 3 Bands of NAPLAN | 94.7% | 95.2% | | |
| Net Promoter Score of Schools | 42.8% | 42.8% | | |
| Net Promoter Score of Resources | 32.8% | 32.7% | | |
| Outcome Score (Multiplication of Denominator) | 8.72 | 9.22 | 0.50 | 5.7% |
| State Funding (recurrent ex. Capex) | $7,938,916,780.74 | $8,416,456,533.00 | $477,539,752.26 | 6.0% |
| Federal Funding (recurrent ex. Capex) | $3,791,729,508.20 | $3,948,891,000.00 | $157,161,491.80 | 4.1% |
| Total Funding | $11,730,646,288.93 | $12,365,347,533.00 | $634,701,244.07 | 5.4% |
| Residential population | 6,097,599 | 6,244,227 | 146,628 | 2.4% |
| Annual cost of education per citizen | $1,923.81 | $ 1,980.28 | $56.47 | 2.9% |

Figure 3: Worked Example – Victorian Schools

Just like Sam and Daisy's investment, a one-year result is far more meaningful and informative when we can compare performance over multiple years. Many investment cases take time to yield results, and only by comparing results over an extended period can we truly gauge relative performance. Below is how we might apply this measure over successive years:

| Victorian Schools | 2015 | 2016 | Change | % Change |
|---|---|---|---|---|
| 10-12 Retention Rates | 84.8% | 85.0% | | |
| 7-12 retention Rates | 86.4% | 87.9% | | |
| Year 12 Attainment Rates | 89.5% | 92.6% | | |
| % of Students Achieving top 3 Bands of NAPLAN | 94.7% | 95.2% | | |
| Net Promoter Score of Schools | 42.8% | 42.8% | | |
| Net Promoter Score of Resources | 32.8% | 32.7% | | |
| Outcome Score (Multiplication of Denominator) | 8.72 | 9.22 | 0.50 | 5.7% |
| State Funding (recurrent ex. Capex) | $7,938,916,780.74 | $8,416,456,533.00 | $477,539,752.26 | 6.0% |
| Federal Funding (recurrent ex. Capex) | $3,791,729,508.20 | $3,948,891,000.00 | $157,161,491.80 | 4.1% |
| Total Funding | $11,730,646,288.93 | $12,365,347,533.00 | $634,701,244.07 | 5.4% |
| Residential population | 6,097,599 | 6,244,227 | 146,628 | 2.4% |
| Annual cost of education per citizen | $1,923.81 | $ 1,980.28 | $56.47 | 2.9% |

Figure 3: Worked Example – Victorian Schools

In the example above, a 5.7% increase in educational outcomes in 2016 compared with 2015 came at an additional cost of $635m, or a 5.4% increase in funding. This is then offset by population growth, so the cost per citizen increased by $56.47, or a 2.9% increase in cost per citizen. It is then up to the public to judge if a 5.7% increase in outcomes is a good return on the 2.9% increase in cost, but at least they are more informed than simply evaluating the total dollars spent.

If outcomes went up whilst spending went down, then the performance would be significantly improved, whilst if outcomes went down but spending went up, then this would be a poor return on taxpayer funds, for which the government should be held accountable.

*Surely that is a bit simplistic?*

When sharing this idea with decision-makers, I tend to receive overall support, but the following legitimate concerns:

1. These might not be the right measures
2. Nobody will understand the calculations
3. This just replicates what the Productivity Commission does
4. Bureaucrats will just manipulate the numbers to suit themselves

No measurement is perfect, but at least a Return on Taxpayer Investment (RTI) model provides increased transparency, debate, and accountability. Just like the Consumer Price Index, most don't understand the calculation and even fewer calculate it, but we all have a reaction when it rises from 3%

to 8%. In the same manner, the RTI calculation is complex and indicative, but at least it is digestible and directionally helpful.

The Productivity Commission does a thorough and rigorous job, and perhaps the natural place for such measurement and tracking is the Productivity Commission. However, if you were to ask the average voter how helpful they feel the Commission's findings have assisted the public, they may struggle to come up with an answer. In my experience, the rigour of the commission provides a density that is not easily digestible beyond senior bureaucrats and academics, which perhaps is its target audience.

Whether or not the government, or an independent body such as a think-tank or accounting firm, is best placed to develop such a measure is unclear. Regardless, the media would no doubt be most interested in the idea of increased transparency and measurement on which to highlight government performance in a manner that can be more easily digested by the public.

Regardless of these challenges, any measure that holds decision-makers accountable for spending public funds beyond "the party that spends the most, cares the most" is a step in the right direction. We shouldn't abandon measurement because it's not perfect, otherwise, we'd abolish weather forecasts. Even an imperfect measure would focus voters and decision-makers. Surely our taxpayers deserve some sort of feedback on how their investments have performed. It's a matter of trust.

About the author: Robert Holt is a Managing Director in the Public Service sector at Accenture and has previously worked in strategy consulting, private equity, finance and law.

# 8

# Tilting at Windmills: Government delusion as the hero in Australia's future prosperity

## Gisele Kapterian

The great challenge currently dominating our national discourse manifests as an economic one: it is an uncomfortable combination of rising inflation rates, rising energy prices, housing affordability issues and significant government debt largely driven by the pandemic. However, the challenge starts and ends as a social and political one - a question about our values and whom we aspire to be. Our nation's greatest comparative advantage has been our measured freedom manifested in both markets and mindsets. It is unfettered thinking, coupled with incentive and opportunity that are the heart, soul, and backbone of our nation's success and, indeed, that of many western democracies. However, recent government responses suggest the greatest threat to our future prosperity lies in the delusion that government can and should cast itself in the lead role of our economy – the Don Quixote of prosperity. History has shown that only a free market with limited government involvement will produce the solutions to the challenges we face.

The timeless tale of *Don Quixote* holds several useful lessons for us as we emerge from the pandemic. On one hand, the story is one of aspiration, of dreaming big dreams and refusing to be limited by the circumstances into which we might be born. Miguel de Cervantes Saavedra pondered "When life itself seems lunatic, who knows where madness lies? Perhaps to be too practical is madness... .and maddest of all: to see life as it is, and not as it should be!"

As we confront the issues before us, we will need to be innovative. And we will need to be deliberate in the methods we choose if we want the outcomes to be both sustainable and consistent with our nation's values and ambitions. It's timely to recall that it has been the primacy of the principles of free trade that have supported great ideas in western democracies - creating and innovating to overcome not only the basic challenges of the human condition like disease, hunger, warmth, energy and security, but also to create moments of joy, opportunity and prosperity. It is the freedom provided by a capitalist economy that allows for people's needs to be heard, understood, and met most efficiently and effectively. Put simply, ideas cannot flourish in an environment of state control and good ideas can't do good in a distorted market where need, effect and response are muddled by the interference of the state. It is only when freedom exists - in the market and our lives - that ideas allow us to turn life from something it is to something we want it to be.

Given the level of government intervention across all aspects of Australian life during the pandemic, it is perhaps unsurprising that many believe government should lead us out of the current inflationary challenges. However, the skewed outcomes and unintended consequences of countless government-driven programmes (pink bats, school halls, aspects of JobKeeper), remind us of the other poignant lesson Miguel de Cervantes bestows us: the danger of self-delusion. Filling his head with tales of chivalry, our protagonist, Don Quixote, casts himself as the knight-errant in his epic and sets out to right the wrongs of the world. What ensues is a series of misadventures fuelled by the misalignment of belief and reality. Problems were created where none existed, and our hero wastes his energy tilting at windmills.

Similarly, the government must avoid the paternalistic delusion that it knows better than our communities of business and enterprise. This is because the free market allows businesses to not only bear the consequences of poor decisions through financial losses but adjust quickly when this happens. Government has neither the incentives to change course quickly, nor does it face immediate consequences for bad business decisions. This leaves the taxpayer to foot the bill not only for the term of the policy but its long-term consequences as well.

So, what gives businesses the ability to read the market better than well-intentioned albeit quixotic governments? Put simply, prices. Prices, as the economist Thomas Sowell states, are like "messengers conveying news". Those prices alert sellers to supply, consumer demand, and efficiencies. They are also sensitive, allowing for early detection of misallocated resources.

This means that when the government chooses to take the lead role on prices to right perceived wrongs in pursuit of its vision of what society should look like, we stifle the indicators of demand and supply, and lose the creator of efficiency. Monty Python's famous 'hearing aid' sketch springs to mind in which the customer's need was not satisfied because of the misunderstanding of the request.

The case for the primacy of the principles of free trade is made starkly in Australia's quest for energy security in this era of transition. If managed correctly, Australia could emerge as a renewable energy superpower, with significant economic, environmental and security advantages that would boost its international influence, diminish its dependencies on nations that do not share its values and create more jobs locally in industries that have a future.

Australia already is an energy superpower being one of the world's largest exporters of coal, uranium and liquified natural gas (LNG). However, this mantle has been won through a 'dig it and ship it philosophy that fails to nurture the development of higher-value domestic industries and has done little to capitalise on arguably our most powerful comparative advantage: Australian ingenuity. Our creative approach to problem-solving has manifested in several world-leading innovations, including the black box flight recorder, Wi-Fi, spray-on skin for burn victims, and the technology behind Google Maps. Our track record in the renewable energy space is also impressive and includes the Passivated Emitter and Rear Cell (PERC), developed at the University of New South Wales, which has supercharged efficiency rates for solar panels and is projected to power approximately half the world's solar power. Technology, investment, and demand can do a great many things if the market is free enough to incentivise good thinking. We are seeing similar developments in nuclear power generation in the United States.

More significant for our nation's renewables transition are the economic circumstances currently manifesting. If we accept that there is both a significant economic and security benefit for our nation in moving to renewables, let alone an environmental one, with the potential for our nation to be a price setter rather than a price taker when it comes to energy, then it would be counterintuitive for government to intervene today and directly regulate the price of gas. This is because the increased price of gas (inflamed by the invasion of Ukraine) would incentivise consumers to use less of it, further encouraging the uptake of renewables and sending positive signals to the investor market to continue to invest and innovate in new technologies.

However, the reality Australia faces is that the transition to renewable sources of energy will continue to take time. The government would do better to address supply issues for gas in the short term – the price of which would still be influenced by geopolitics and the global directional shift to renewables - rather than engage in the indelicate task of price fixing.

What would happen if the government were to succumb to the temptation of donning its suit of armour (imagine a pasteboard taped to a helmet to fashion a visor) and take the lead on gas prices? When government interferes in the price of traded goods, history has proven the consequences: investment is stifled, jobs are jeopardised, and, if that price is set too high, our exports become uncompetitive, and if set too low, our exports are exposed to retaliatory measures by importing countries. This is particularly so when it relates to a production input as critical and ubiquitous as energy. More immediately, the viability of domestic operations is reassessed, as the cost to do business locally becomes less advantageous than in other markets. This puts both jobs and our local gas supply at risk.

Governments don't have to search long to find examples of how best intentions exercised through market interference create perverse outcomes. One of history's most notable is what Horst Sibert coined "the Cobra Effect". To reduce Delhi's deadly cobra population, the British offered payment for every dead cobra. While the programme was initially successful, enterprising locals quickly responded to the situation by breeding more cobras. Once authorities realised this, the payment quickly ceased. Cobra breeders now had no reason to keep their stocks and released them in their now greater numbers, further exacerbating an already bad situation.

We are on the brink of our cobra effect moment here. Price controls on fossil fuels would undoubtedly create a market distortion that, even when lifted, will have robbed our nation of the crucial time and necessary circumstances to not only encourage energy transition but also support a local renewable energy industry that could have enormous potential for our nation as a leader in the fuels of the future. Without government price intervention, the rise in the price of gas would see consumers and investors look at options that are less costly, less vulnerable to supply challenges, and less regulated.

The current trade wars over semiconductors are also a stark

reminder of how we should go about supporting any fledgling renewable energy industry in Australia. Over the last 40 years, the manufacturing of the world's semiconductors has moved from the United States and Europe to East Asia. The disruptions of the pandemic and war made the west's dependency more apparent - especially given semiconductors are now as essential as energy to both consumer and defence technologies. So, in 2022, the United States introduced a host of legislation aiming to distort the market in favour of encouraging the manufacturing of semiconductors back to America. This tool kit is made up of significant subsidies and export controls and has now set the scene for a problematic 'race to the bottom'.

It is important to note a part of the reason the United State and Europe lost these industries in the first place was because of state involvement. Higher levels of regulation for inputs and red tape combined with comparatively higher taxes in Europe and the United States made a compelling case for moving businesses to where the cost of running them was cheaper - even if the know-how resided elsewhere. Some of the economies trying to lure the semiconductor industry also put on the table significant direct subsidies as well as subsidised energy inputs. While some may argue this strategy seems like a great way to create industries, the wins are temporary. Heavy subsidies work for a limited time only if these economies find other markets to export to and can push out the local competition. Significantly, they do so even at the expense of higher quality products which in turn stymies the development of efficiencies and new capabilities, ultimately depriving the market and consumer of a better product on both price and functionality. The cost to the state and thus the taxpayer is also significant because it means finite resources that could have been allocated to more beneficial ends were squandered on an unsustainable strategy.

Australia's agriculture industry has shown how better products outperform highly subsidised ones. The OECD average producer support was 18.5% of gross farm receipts from 2016 to 2018. In the United States producer support sat at around 10% and in Australia, that support was only 2% for the same period. And yet, Australia has a far more export-oriented agriculture industry compared with the United States, exporting approximately 70% of its produce compared with 20% from the United States. It's Australia's high-value agricultural products that make it a successful exporter, able to compete exceedingly well in the most sophisticated consumer markets. As Professor Patrick Boyle has noted, "you don't win a race by trying to trip your opponent up, especially when there are significant costs to doing so. A far better strategy is to run faster."

Of course, the government has also not been absent from renewable power adoption in Australia. Some could argue that given the rapid increase in price efficiencies - for example, solar photovoltaic dropping by over 80% per megawatt hour in the decade even after subsidies applied in certain countries are accounted for - this should mean that renewables are now able to sit alongside all other forms of energy, unaided by government support, and compete purely on what makes the most sense to the end consumer. Others would argue that due to the climate crisis, support is required to accelerate the adoption that would have occurred regardless.

While the government would do well to avoid auditioning for the lead role in markets, when it comes to economic policy, the government's greatest value lies in its ability to create a framework supporting ingenuity and enterprise. Investing in research and development, encouraging the local development of, and migration of people with the right skills, supporting industry and academia to work more closely and reducing red tape. In addition to the carrot, this role also requires a stick as market freedom is not absolute - disincentivising and regulating anti-competitive behaviours, like monopolies, predatory pricing and dumping, are crucial to ensuring the market continues to do what it does best: respond effectively and efficiently to what the people want, demand or need. In maintaining this framework, government plays its role in prosperity, knowing this is the best way to secure the resources for those in our society who need help.

As Australia fronts into the latest economic headwinds, it is more important than ever to remember the foundation of freedom that has made our nation a success to date. As Margaret Thatcher stated "A [person]'s right to work as [they] will, to spend what [they] earn, to own property, to have the State as a servant and not as master... they are the essence of a free economy. And on that freedom, all our other freedoms depend."

*Gisele Kapterian is the Senior Director of Public Sector Strategy for Salesforce APAC. She has previously worked as a lawyer and as an adviser in the federal parliament.*

# 9

# We should be so lucky

## Andrew Low

Unlike most of its region, Australia was left unscathed by the Asian crash of 1997. Unlike most of the developed world, it shrugged off the global financial crisis and unlike most commodity-exporting countries, it weathered the resources bust too. No other rich country has ever managed to grow so steadily for so long. By that measure, at least, Australia boasts the world's most successful economy.

*The Economist*, October 2018

As the delegates gathered for the constitutional conventions that determined how the colonies would come together as a country, they were buoyed by the knowledge that a united Australia would be the richest country in the world, measured by wealth per person. Convicts had given way to a wave of free immigrants in the middle of the nineteenth century and foreign investment streamed into the colonies. At the same time, the repeal of the Corn Laws in Britain launched half a century of unprecedented free trade and world peace. Australia, replete with sheep and gold and possessing a liberal trading ethic, took full advantage of the opportunity.

By the time Donald Horne wrote *The Lucky Country* in the 1960s, though, Australia was three-quarters of the way through a slump in the relative economic success that took the country down from first to fourteenth in the world. It was a slow and almost imperceptible decline over 80 years as a result of several well-meaning but flawed decisions made in the early years of the twentieth century that Paul Kelly has collectively dubbed "the Australian Settlement". As he articulated in his book *The End of Certainty*, the newly federated states adopted a consensus to protect Australian companies from global competition, by applying tariffs on imports, and protect Australian workers from competition, through the White Australia policy and a centralised wage-fixing conciliation and arbitration process.

Horne conveys the impact of this world in which "to many Australian businessmen the way to make money is to grab some ideas from overseas, rush them into operation, however inefficiently, and then rely on the Tariff Board for protection. The central occupation of manufacturing is often to kill overseas competition with high tariffs." Australians have forgotten the impact of that approach, but it is timely to recall it at a time when protectionism is making a comeback in most developed countries and many others too. A retreat from globalisation could again drive the negative impacts on living standards of that not-so-long-ago time in Australia when "there was no particular need to be efficient or to worry about world standards. . . but with making profits by putting pressure on the Tariff Board or by collusive practices with their competitors".

There is much of Horne's criticism of Australian business

culture that still rings true (a lack of interest in R&D, board conservatism and parochialism, too many businesses coasting on government contracts), but it would be too harsh to still say, as he did in the 1960s, that "there is still talk of free enterprise in Australia but to many manufacturers, this is just a lesson they have learned off by heart without understanding. . . Often what it means is that the business man (sic) demands from the government a special protection that will help him continue to survive". Far fewer Australian businesses now lean solely on government largesse to survive, and most now compete confidently and profitably in global markets, including some of the world's leaders in areas from shopping centre development to infrastructure finance and medical technologies. Technology companies are now the fastest growing sector and the subsidies provided to these companies (in the form of R&D credits) don't rely on protection from competition or governments trying to pick individual 'winners' for their effect.

Though the weaning of Australia from the sins of the early twentieth century happened in stages throughout the second half of the century, the conventional wisdom is correct when we say that Australia turned the corner in the 1980s. The reforms of that period and the further gains made in the 1990s are well documented and have put Australia back on top as the wealthiest country in the world, measured by the median wealth of its people.

Indeed, out of the 193 countries recognised by the United Nations, Australia is only the 55th largest in population but ranks thirteenth for the size of the economy and tenth for GDP per person (the average wealth is below the median wealth because wealth in Australia is more evenly distributed than in the nine countries that have higher averages but who have more concentration at the top). There was an inflection point when Australia lost its way at the start of the 20$^{th}$ century and a time when it was rediscovered in the 80s and 90s.

Australians are often complacent about this economic success, thinking that it will continue regardless and even sometimes undervaluing the whole idea of growth. It's easy to disparage material comforts as unexciting and boring, and true that many other things (family or sports and culture) underpin the well-lived life. But it's equally true that a strong economy underpins the investments we make in everything else we value. The security of the country, a family's standard of living and resilience, and the healthcare and social welfare system; all those things require a strong economy. Australia has only been able to lead the world in making an unprecedented level of investment in things like disability care and mental health because the country generates enough economic growth to fund it.

When economic success does get acknowledged it's usually put down to a temporary dose of blind luck (iron ore being the usual example). The assumption is that you can still say today, as Horne did fifty years ago, that the Australian economy is underpinned by being resource rich and able to surf off the back of offshore innovation. Not true. The last 30 years have certainly seen a long China-driven boom in commodity prices, but it's been a rollercoaster along the way. Resource exports were 11% of GDP in 2011 and then 5% in 2015 and yet economic growth held steady, while other major countries with big resources exports, such as Brazil, South Africa, and even Canada, went into recession.

The 'coasting on the coattails of resources' thesis doesn't adequately explain 30 years without a recession. It also stands in contrast to the evidence in numerous international studies that, counter-intuitively, those countries with more resources usually have lower economic growth than those that are less well-endowed. This has been dubbed the 'resources curse' and compared with the difficulties that commonly affect lottery winners struggling to manage the side effects of sudden and unpredictable wealth. Resource wealth is typically either captured by a small group of people or appropriated by the government for the benefit of wasteful rent seekers. Norway, with its sovereign wealth fund, is one of the only other examples of not wasting commodity-driven income. Australians aren't rich just (or even mainly) because of the bounty of resource wealth in the ground.

The true reason for sustaining economic growth through the cycles is the longstanding but underestimated Australian flexibility, discipline and adaptability - plus the newfound resilience built in through the eighties and nineties. The reforms of the 1980s (and to a lesser extent since then) fundamentally transformed what Horne recognised in the 1960s was holding back the country and, even where it may have had some benefits, had outlived its relevance. In the characteristically blunt words of Paul Keating at Bob Hawke's memorial service, "Australia's creativity had been locked down by a stultifying paternal policy regime – the idea that government knew best and that Australia was best protected and nurtured as a closed economy." In the same way, as it did for China after 1979 and more recently for Vietnam and increasingly also India, an opening to the world and to freeing of markets allowed a once rigid Australia to become adaptive and capable of sustainably higher growth rates than before.

Australians will need to be careful not to squander this from geopolitical fears or fading memories of the reasons for reform. Surveys show a lot of younger people don't trust the market economy and find socialism more appealing. One reason for this is that anyone under forty has no memory of the sclerosis that existed in our societies before the liberal economic reforms of the eighties – the Winter of Discontent in the United Kingdom and the pre-reform rigidity and deficiencies of Australia in the seventies – and economic history is not well taught in schools and universities. Another reason is that there have been some appalling abuses that have given business a bad name, from the crony capitalism of firms using money and lobbyists to rig markets and create anti-competitive monopolies (especially in the United States) to multinational tax avoidance and the bad behaviour outlined in Australia's Banking Royal Commission. If business does not act in a way that's worthy of people's trust, isn't ethical or undermines fair and transparent markets, then it's no surprise that people turn against capitalism. The consequences for prosperity are serious.

I had an early lesson in this when I travelled through the old Soviet Union in the first few months after the fall of the Berlin Wall. The Communists were still in control, but it was becoming more and more clear that the system had not worked and most people in the Eastern Bloc were desperate to enjoy the things we took for granted in the West. I had lots of offers for Levi's, and everywhere I went there were long queues for a limited range of things to buy, often quirky because the central planners had decided to produce more of something than people wanted to buy and less of something else. That year, cucumbers were in over-supply but milk and eggs were scarce. The longest queue was outside the newly opened first McDonald's in Moscow, where I queued for half an hour while being offered a chance to avoid the queue by buying 'black market' McDonald's that was being passed out the back of the restaurant for sale to foreigners at ten times the price. That's how it works without clear and transparent competitive markets to match what people want to buy with what they want to sell.

When I got to Warsaw the people were a bit happier and there was more food in the shops. As control from Moscow receded, people eagerly started to trade with each other. Finally, I crossed into West Berlin from the eastern side and it was like going from a black-and-white movie into a Technicolor one. From a bleak land of scarcity to a rich and modern city, from tinny Trabants to new Mercedes. As with North and South Korea (another border I later had the chance to visit), the gap between East and West Germany provided the perfect natural experiment to test a market-driven economy against a socialist economy in the same land and culture. My experiences drove home the importance of teaching about Germany and Korea and about the different phases of our history, including the time Australia embraced protectionism and cronyism, leading to stagnation, and when the country opened itself up.

More than 20 years later when I was studying how China had grown from poverty to being many times the size of Australia (while having my on-the-ground tutorial through hundreds of trips to a dozen Chinese Provinces), it became clear that the same thing drove China's 'economic miracle'. First, the government allowed a few farmers in the collective to sell any extra food they produced. Those farms suddenly produced much more and the programme was extended further. Then the government allowed small privately owned businesses to be created in a special economic zone in Shenzhen which also led to dramatic growth. Most of China's leaders were engineers by training in those days, so they set up more pilot projects to test the use of markets in different parts of the economy and extended the ones that worked until the whole country had markets working to some degree or another.

As one China scholar has put it: the Communist Party likes to credit itself with 'lifting millions out of poverty' but it is more accurate to say that the millions lifted the Party. Entrepreneurial, hard-working and smart Chinese people built amazing businesses and created wealth on a scale never seen before. Key technocrats and leaders like Premier Zhu Rongji deserve credit for the way they allowed this to happen in the 40 years from 1979 but their main accomplishment was to improve education and infrastructure, open China to international trade and investment and then get out of the way of the ordinary Chinese people whose energy fuelled China's growth (assisted by the globalisation trend where the other countries of the world opened up to Chinese exports and foreign investment flowed into China).

In the last few years, there has unfortunately been a relapse into trying to 'manage' markets more tightly by the State (with negative consequences that will continue to play out over time) but in the meantime, China has achieved a velocity of growth and innovation that have become at least partially self-sustaining. Ironically, many people around the world have imagined China's growth to show that there is some new growth recipe of 'State-driven capitalism' when the truth is actually that the growth of China for about 30 years was a perfect example of Adam Smith's "invisible hand" – of markets allocating resources more productively than a central authority could. China's growth has not been qualitatively different in its drivers to other Asian 'tiger markets', it's just happened on a remarkably larger scale in a country with 10 to 500 times as many people.

Using markets when they work should not be regarded as a right-wing agenda. It's true that flexible labour markets and a floating dollar are important as shock absorbers that allow us to adapt. Keeping public debt low, having an attractive regime for foreign investment and encouraging skilled immigration have been crucial for Australian success. But so also have universal healthcare through Medicare, compulsory superannuation savings to redress the previous 'savings gap' in Australia and allowing university students to pay for their education only much later when they earn enough to do so. Having the OECD's highest minimum wage has not prevented the Australian unemployment rate from getting down to 3%. People who are more easily able to change jobs, move house and keep educating themselves and their children are going to be much better able to move rapidly from areas of the economy that are slumping to those that are growing.

There was much gnashing of teeth in 2019 when a Harvard study group ranked Australia's index of Economic Complexity behind those of Botswana and Uganda. The Harvard Atlas of Economic Complexity ranks Australia very poorly for the diversity and complexity of our exports. They claim that countries that make more products and compete in more areas in their exports are more sophisticated and will grow more. Australia does badly in this measure because resources (and tourism and education, pre-pandemic) represent such a large proportion of our exports, and manufactured products are less prevalent. The Australian lack of confidence was quickly on display when the ranking was published; Australia is 'rich but dumb and getting dumber' screamed the headlines in fear.

It is the Harvard Atlas that is simplistic, rather than the Australian economy. Firstly, the notion of 'resources' as a 'dumb' export does not recognise the high-tech automation and world-leading efficiencies and safety of the modern mining industry, from autonomous train loading to automated underground mining systems. It also doesn't pick up the sheer range of minerals (from lithium to rare earths to uranium and platinum) that Australia produces and how flexibly and efficiently investment can toggle between each new mineral and efficiently finance their development. Australia sells resources, tourism and education (not properly picked up in the Harvard Atlas) because the country is particularly competitive at doing so and the biggest consumers of these things are proximate. That's what Ricardo called "comparative advantage", and Australia remains a great example of its power to fuel prosperity.

The Harvard Atlas definition of 'productive knowledge' also doesn't account for the workforce. McKinsey has estimated that almost half of Australian jobs are 'interaction jobs' that require high-order reasoning, judgement and the ability to manage non-routine tasks. Australia's skilled labour is above global averages and performs even more strongly than Japan (which ranks first in Harvard Atlas' economic complexity measure) when it comes to 'complex problem solving'. More than two-thirds of people in the Australian mining sector have advanced-level degrees or diplomas.

There is nothing wrong with an Australian Government highlighting emerging industries where they think Australia has potential, as they've done with health & life sciences, cyber & defence, space, clean energy and food & agricultural technologies. But it will take discipline to promote these only with the policies that we know do work (like creating 'precincts' and 'centres of excellence' that link into educational institutions to create critical mass and giving visas liberally to talented people from around the world who have those skills) and not with policies that don't work (like subsidies for the more articulate lobbyists among what government or bureaucrats deem to be 'future industries').

Australians often don't even recognise their comparative economic efficiencies as they aren't things that manufacturing-centric economists naturally think about. The dividend imputation system stops the double-taxation of dividends paid by companies in the hands of their investors and, in so doing, encourages companies not only to pay their taxes but to distribute any cash for which they don't have a compelling investment need. The allocation of capital among companies is more efficient as a result and the higher overall returns (including those dividends) to shareholders in Australia than in other markets shows it. Entry to Australian Universities has been meritocratic like in China or Singapore: State-wide exams anonymously marked and scaled to reflect the relative difficulties of courses with places allocated 'blind' based on the resulting score. They therefore better train the people most capable of benefiting from higher education, rather than losing good students to those with well-connected parents, particular racial background (as in Malaysia who leaks talent to Australian Universities) or the ability to smooth-talk their way through an interview.

Australian capital markets raise new equity for half the cost of the United States and recapitalise companies through innovative structures like accelerated rights offerings that reconcile equal treatment for shareholders with speed and transparency. Almost all houses in Australia are sold by auction and detailed house-by-house valuation comparisons and online search are available, whereas, in most parts of the world, there is an opaque and less market-based approach to pricing. These aren't the things that jump to the mind of economists, let alone others, when we think about efficiency, but they underpin long-term productivity just as much as the more talked-about labour market and other efficiencies.

Australia also has one of the few AAA credit ratings in the world (recently confirmed after Covid, while many other countries were down-graded) and a unique set of free trade agreements with the United States, China, Japan, the United Kingdom and India – to which the European Union is likely to be soon added – giving Australian businesses preferential access to 90% of the world. Australian attitudes to free trade have more in common with the dynamic economies of Asia than with other more fearful and protectionist countries in what is identified as 'the West'. The more robust Australian anti-monopoly regime has preserved competition more than the United States system despite (or because) a smaller market more naturally tends towards oligopoly and a succession of strong competition regulators have pushed back on excessive concentration and dilution of competition. Australian venture capital funding for start-up companies tripled in the last 5 years and that doesn't include the increasing amount of attention from Silicon Valley on Australian companies.

The story of Australia's revival in the 80s and 90s has been told before. But if it is drowned out by the demand for reshoring and 'clever' funds to create 'future industry' then Australia no longer has the right national narrative that can keep the success going. The successful return to growth and high employment within a year of Covid added a fourth story of superior economic resilience to the three cited in the quote from *The Economist* at the start of this chapter. But many Australians, companies and individuals, did get used to 'free money' during a year and a half of unprecedented and somewhat undiscriminating financial support. Lobbyists for a pre-1980s industrial policy have been emboldened to re-emerge in sexier packaging. Australians will need to be very vigilant not to give away hard-won gains.

Saul Eslake has also pointed out that even the long-term closing of Australia's borders for multiple years was a form of protection in the same way as tariffs were in Donald Horne's time. Like tariffs, locking out people and investment provides a temporary sugar hit as local companies and people looking for work don't have foreign competition, but as time goes on Australia becomes less and less competitive, new ideas go elsewhere and new industries that require skills not available locally just never get built or get set up at much higher cost.

As well as resisting a slide back to the Sixties and Seventies, Australia needs continuous improvement – what the Japanese call *kaizen* – to keep tweaking the settings and stay adaptable as the world changes. We have demonstrated within my lifetime that we are capable of doing it. At different times in our history, both major political parties have shown the ability to drive this sort of incremental change that encourages resilience. It is not a matter of having grand plans for the government to 'solve' everything from Climate Change to Poverty. Perhaps the only truly successful 'moonshot' was the eponymous American mission to put a man on the moon in the Sixties (where the technologies existed but just needed funding and political will to be harnessed). Most attempts at 'moonshots' just end up costing a lot of money for indifferent results; think of the centralised 'War' declared on cancer, then drugs, then 'terror', even before you get to government's putting in big new IT systems, building submarines or the Great Leap Forward. Success far more often comes from the accumulation of smaller innovations from multiple parties that compete against each other (think of Covid vaccines and Silicon Valley) and in government policy from the accumulation of many well-thought-through policies, often copied from what's worked overseas.

Several lessons stand out in reviewing the periods in Australia's history where a 'miracle economy' has been achieved and the periods where the country has stalled or gone backwards. The first is that the good periods have seen stability of leadership and some degree of bipartisanship in the national interest. This does not mean that policy debates stop. On the contrary, the contestability of ideas is an absolute strength and it is almost unique that even in wartime Australia continued to have an opposition to challenge the government (unlike in the United Kingdom for example). But it does mean 'playing the ball and not the person', and that once a policy emerges as superior to the alternative it should be supported on principle and not blocked for personal advantage. There will always be a temptation to block things and the media wants fisticuffs, but those politicians who truly care about and represent the Australian national interest will 'give credit where credit is due', or at least fight on the high moral ground rather than the 'easy kill'.

The Prime Minister's party has only controlled the Senate for three of the last 39 years. For much of the time, this ability to veto and block government legislation has been used constructively to amend and selectively challenge in a way that creates better legislation. But there are periods where it's been used in an almost knee-jerk fashion to stalemate. The impact of instinctively negative opposition goes well beyond the specific reforms that don't get through parliament. The greater impact is to discourage any further attempts at reform, to coarsen the public debate, polarise the media and to make voters more cynical about the whole democratic process. It's no exaggeration to say that oppositions have as much power as governments to do good or harm to the country – either to engage constructively and improve legislation or to drive the country away from even attempting improvement.

The successful tax reforms of the eighties and nineties also show the importance of a second principle: balanced reform. The 1985 tax reforms brought new taxes on capital gains and fringe benefits but also a substantial cut in the top marginal tax rate. Even the sceptics could see it was a reform to make things work better rather than just a grab for money. Keating has rightly noted that the reaction to the Labour Party's 2019 policy to eliminate franking credit cash payments and 'negative gearing' tax deductions for property investors might have been quite different if the money saved had been used differently and not given the sense that it was simply designed to slug a particular constituency rather than reform.

The eighties brought successive waves of deregulation, from the float of the dollar and new banks to removing tariffs and then finally abolishing centralised wage-fixing. But in parallel with these critical opening-up reforms to make the economy more competitive there came universal healthcare in the form of Medicare, interest-free HECS loans to ensure affordable university education and setting up the superannuation system. The government made changes that promoted efficiency and economic growth, supported by those on the opposite side of politics, but balanced them carefully with well-chosen policies that would comfort people that their security wasn't being left behind in the deregulatory push. We don't see so much of this approach in recent times, and both parties would benefit from looking at balanced reform proposals across a year and a term of government to offset microeconomic reform (making Australia more competitive and open) with social reform (that protects the potential losers, short or long term, in a more competitive world).

The third lesson is that the extent of advocacy and 'education' is very important. Enduring change came when Hawke, Keating or Howard talked clearly to people, long and hard, about why change was required, and also when bodies like the Productivity Commission and Royal Commissions were able to independently assess changes and give a considered imprimatur. Changes have failed when reforms got rushed without adequate socialising of people affected or where they too narrowly reflected the interest of one part of society (be it Work Choices for the Coalition or the punitive carbon tax that the Greens forced on Labour when a consensus for more market-based carbon pricing existed at the time).

The shaping of institutions is important. You can trace the evolution of the old protectionist Tariff Board to the Industry Assistance Commission in 1974, becoming the Industry Commission in 1989 and then the Productivity Commission in 1998. At each stage, the mandate shifted further away from how to avoid, and compensate people for, competition towards how to be prepared for it and to make sure that both investors in businesses and employees of businesses can maximise the benefits of their respective capital.

It is often argued that its 'too hard' to promote worthwhile reform in Australia today. This comes both from protest movements, who take to the streets in frustration that the machinery of democracy doesn't appear to be delivering racial equality or effectively countering climate change, and also from business who see a stalling of reform and an unwillingness to make worthwhile changes to make Australia more prosperous and competitive. Both would say that social media and the 24-hour media cycle have made it impossible to sustain a mature argument about what's required and that the tendency for the Senate to include minority parties makes it hard to pass legislation. Reform may be hard, but it's certainly not impossible.

Australians are cautious and sceptical and bringing in changes without a lot of explanation and a compelling rationale is therefore always going to fail. You can blame the Senate for not getting corporate tax cuts or you can recognise that a sufficiently compelling case was never made as to why (especially with a dividend imputation system and no shortage of foreign investment) cutting corporate taxes was a better use of government money than alternatives. Contrast that example with how Hawke and Keating developed the case for tax reform in the 1980s via a Summit of all the key stakeholders and years of jawboning. Introducing a GST failed twice, in 1984 and 1991, but the arguments for its necessity had been well made and enough had sunk in for Howard and Costello to make it happen, finally, in 1999. Political boldness is sometimes required, but it needs to build and surf the wave of public understanding rather than try to swim against it. A fair-minded and objective assessment of our history and the Australian character and values does not support the fashionable pessimism of the current consensus that says reform is 'no longer possible'.

In recent decades, mostly sound economic management has made the average Australian richer than the average citizen of every other country in the world. Australia shouldn't throw this away or imagine that some revolutionary change is required. Instead, a methodical and well-articulated programme for continuous improvement will make sure that Australians continue to lead the world in median wealth and prosperity.

*Andrew Low is a Company Director and former Head of Macquarie Capital in Asia and Global Head of Investment Banking for CLSA. This essay is extracted from his forthcoming book "We Should be so Lucky: Why the Australian Way Works".*

# 10

# Reforming our criminal justice system

## Evan Mulholland

I believe the Liberal Party must take back ownership of the conservative value of redemption.

In an age when incarceration rates are rising, it is time to appeal to our better selves, and the good in our fellow citizens, by exploring innovative ways to combat the root causes of crime.

The key task for reform of the criminal justice system is to differentiate between the people we are afraid of, and the people that we are just mad at.

When discussing this policy area, one thing which the ideologues on the left always misunderstand is that to achieve community support for any reform, community safety must always remain the priority. Always.

The bipartisan reform of the justice system can never be achieved if the public does not have confidence in the system to keep dangerous criminals behind bars.

As Liberals, we have a proven track record of keeping the community safe that we should be proud of. However, we should also be honest enough to learn from previous elections that sometimes the 'tough on crime' mantra can go too far.

For those on the right, we should want to see reform for a greater purpose than the left. We must make the case on good policy, not simply ideology, as we so often see from the left.

Reducing high rates of incarceration means a greater number of Australians can become productive members of society. Achieving this through employment, supporting their families and becoming active members of their local communities.

If we abhor 'cancel culture', as we should, we should also apply those same principles to our justice system. People are better than their worst moments. And those who have followed the wrong path should always be helped onto the right one where there is an opportunity to do so.

For too long, the justice portfolio has been quarantined from the smaller government agenda on the Liberal side of politics. But the strain on the prison population, and the growing need to build more prisons, is costing governments billions. That should worry conservatives, classical liberals and libertarians alike.

We know from the Productivity Commission's 2021 report, *The Prison Dilemma*, spending on prisoners and prisons closely aligns with rates of incarceration. Therein lies the growing need for economic conservatives to engage with criminal justice reform.

The numbers consistently seem starker in Victoria. The Productivity Commission found that Victoria had the highest average annual growth in the real level of prison cost from 2011-12 to 2019-20 at 7.3%. Victoria also boasts the highest yearly expenditure per prisoner of any State at $154,000. More than one and a half times the average annual full-time wage.

According to the Sentencing Council of Victoria, Victoria locked up 109 prisoners per 100,000 people in 2021, an increase of 2.1% on 2020. And as of 30 June 2021, Victoria's prison population was 7,248, an increase of 1.4% from the previous year.

While these numbers reflect the government of the day and their approach to the justice and corrections portfolios, they also present an opportunity for reform. We should look at the system as a whole and come up with evidence-based policies to keep people out of prison who should not be there. It is a positive policy reform that would save millions of scarce taxpayer dollars in the process.

New Victorian Liberal Leader John Pesutto sees this as an opportunity. And has appointed Brad Battin to the Liberals' first-ever criminal justice reform portfolio.

As Mr Pesutto has said:

> Finding ways to give young people, especially those growing up in the most disadvantaged of circumstances, the opportunities to pursue a fulfilling and productive life through education, training and employment, will be a key feature of Brad's role.

Developing pathways to ensure that fewer people interact with our justice system is more important than ever.

The Sentencing Council also found 43.6% of prisoners released during 2018–19 returned to Victorian prisons within two years. This rate is slightly lower than the Australian rate of 45.2%. The Northern Territory had the highest rate at 58.9%, and South Australia had the lowest rate at 33.2%.

The rate of people returning to prison following release is not the only measure of recidivism. Another measure of recidivism is the proportion of prisoners who return to corrective services. This measure includes people who return to prison, as well as people who are subsequently placed on community orders.

That number is significantly higher in Victoria at 52.5% in the two years to 2020–21. However, was similar to the national rate of 53.1%.

Victoria has the lowest rate in Australia for community-based sentencing, which represents fine orders, supervision in the community, parole, bail and sentenced probation orders, at 159.2 people per 100,000 adults. Depending on your perspective this can be seen as a positive or a negative. In the United States, Republican States achieved extraordinary success by punishing offenders who were not a threat to the community in alternative ways like community-based orders.

The Institute of Public Affairs, where I was previously employed, recently released a report by the Dean of Law at the Swinburne University of Technology, Professor Mirko Bagaric's, *Australia's Emerging Incarceration Crisis. Proposed Reforms of the Australian Sentencing System*, that found Australia could release almost one-third of its prisoners with little risk to community safety.

According to Professor Bagaric's work, reform proposals should secure the following objectives; crime reduction; appropriate punishment of criminals; minimising the cost of the system; and, ensuring that the system does not violate important moral norms.

To improve the sentencing system, Professor Bagaric wrote it is necessary to reassess the current aims of sentencing; give content to the principle of proportionality; harmonise aggravating and mitigating considerations, establish standard penalties for key offence types and introduce new criminal sanctions.

As Professor Bagaric said:

> The model is loosely based on the systems in Scandinavian countries. The prospect of lowering crime rates and reducing prison numbers is achievable. The imprisonment rate in Scandinavian countries is half of that in Australia and the victimisation rate is less by a factor of approximately one-third. A proportionality-focused sentencing system driven by empirical data can confer profound benefits to the community, in the form of a fairer and less expensive sentencing system and safer community.

Federal Labor Assistant Minister, the Hon Andrew Leigh MP, has been a long-term advocate for criminal justice reform in Australia. In a speech to the Australian Institute of Criminology in October 2022, Dr Leigh pointed out that Australia's incarceration rate has doubled since 1985, despite a dramatic fall in the number of serious offences like murder, car theft and robbery.

Dr Leigh says that stricter policing, tougher sentencing and more stringent bail laws are the main drivers of prison population growth, calculating that governments could have saved $2.6 billion if incarceration had remained at 1985 levels.

The easiest thing to do as a conservative is just to accept that anyone who critiques the current trajectory of the justice system in Australia as 'soft on crime'. What might be more difficult for some is to acknowledge that Dr Leigh has a point.

Framing is key. Dr Leigh is right to pursue criminal justice reform as an economic issue because it is. If you frame reform as saving the taxpayer billions of dollars, you are much more likely to win over a larger share of the population.

The book *Prison Break: Why conservatives turned against mass incarceration* by John Hopkins University academics Dr David Dagan and Associate Professor Steven M. Teles provides extraordinary insight into how Republicans, over time, went from tough of crime, to smart on crime.

Grover Norquist, head of Americans for Tax Reform, and influential Republican intellectual said, as far back as 2011, that criminal justice is conservative's "Last Sacred Cow". Norquist said:

> Spending more on education doesn't necessarily get you more education. We know that – that's obvious. That's also true about criminal justice and fighting crime.

Newt Gingrich made an incredible personal policy reversal on criminal justice reform, once an advocate for using the 'tough on crime' mantra in congressional races, in 2011 he acknowledged that:

> There is an urgent need to address the astronomical growth in the prison population, with its huge costs in dollars and lost human potential. The criminal justice system is broken, and conservatives must lead the way in fixing it.

Former Texas Governor Rick Perry has triumphed corrections reforms as a signature accomplishment, he reflected:

> One of the most important things we did in Texas while I was governor is reform our drug-related sentencing laws, so that non-

violent offenders could stay out of prison.

Perry successfully made the case for "second chances and human redemption".

The legacy of the reform effort in Texas has been the closing of 10 prisons in the past decade, and the prison population has dropped by 17,000, saving the taxpayer tens of millions of dollars.

Perry was late to the party though, and a lot of credit must go to people like criminal justice reformer, and former Republican representative Jerry Madden, who was one of the first to champion a lot of these reforms.

Madden has said Democrats tend to focus on changing lives. Republicans such as him tend to focus on saving money and cutting taxes. So started a bipartisan reform effort. As Madden said:

> I'm a conservative politician who's saying let's save taxpayers some money, but if I can change things so crime goes in a different direction, then I can in fact change lives. If I could do that at the same time as saving money and spending smarter, wouldn't that be a great thing?

We should be looking to these successful criminal justice reform efforts like those in largely Republican states in America like Texas and Georgia, where they have prioritised community safety, given people a second chance at life through alternative punishment and work programs, keeping people out of prison for good, and received a fiscal dividend through being able to close prisons, rather than open new ones.

The key to achieving this was by differentiating those who are a threat to the community, and those who are not. We must draw a clear line in the sand between violent and non-violent offenders.

As a matter of principle, I believe low-level drug possession, defaulting on fines and even some white-collar crime should not be valid reasons for Victorians going to prison.

If they are not a threat to community safety, then they do not belong in prison.

That does not mean that these crimes should go unpunished. We can, and must, prioritise community safety, and also find alternative punishments for people that should not be in prison.

We know that it is far more rational economically to spend a nominal amount, say $100,000 or so, at the start of someone's interaction with the justice system to rehabilitate them, including substance treatment and educational programs, than spend upwards of $150,000 a year, every year for the rest of their life, to keep them in prison.

It is a proposition that makes sound economic sense, but it is importantly, a better outcome for society.

As has been put to practice in the United States, this means money saved on keeping people out of prison, can then be invested in rehabilitating citizens, and ensuring serious violent and sexual offences are punished appropriately in our criminal justice system.

Finding good in people, and rehabilitating them towards a better life, is not a progressive idea. It is a conservative one. We cede ground over compassion to the left at our peril.

The left uses the mirage of compassion as a blunt force to make government bigger, and people less free.

One only has to see how the Black Lives Matter movement in the United States morphed into the 'abolish the police' movement, which has proven a monumental failure.

As Liberals, we should be reluctant to use mechanisms that take away the power of judges to make proportionate sentences. This is why on principle, as a personal view, I do not agree with the use of mandatory minimum sentences. However, it is blatantly clear, on too many occasions, the decisions of courts have simply been out of line with community expectations. But I don't believe proper criminal justice reform is possible with so many clogged in our justice system.

Campaigns in Australia like 'raise the age' which seeks to raise the age of criminal responsibility to 14, in the same way, take power away from our courts to decide the proportionate punishment. Some of the most hideous murders and sexual offences have been carried out by those between the ages of 10-14.

Judges and courts should decide the proportionality of the offence, especially if that individual is a threat to community safety. This ongoing conversation requires a level of discussion far greater than slogans.

This is why the Liberal side of politics should engage in a broad ongoing discussion about criminal justice reform.

A solution to the 'raise the age' policy debate, just might lie in following what reformers in the United States were able to achieve. This could involve differentiating violent and non-violent offences for those aged 10-14. If someone has committed a serious violent offence, then they are a threat to the community and should not be allowed to walk free purely based on their age.

Likewise, if a 10–14-year-old has committed a non-violent offence, this means they are not a threat to community safety and should be punished in other ways. In addition, it is in our economic interest to ensure that the state provides the necessary rehabilitation programs to prevent them from becoming repeat offenders.

I firmly believe there are good human qualities in every Victorian, even those that have followed the wrong path. We should always seek out the good in our fellow Victorians and find a pathway to redemption.

Criminal justice reform should be seriously engaged with by Liberals, it not only makes sound economic sense, but it is also morally the right thing to do.

*Evan is a Member of the Legislative Council in the Parliament of Victoria. Before that he worked for the Institute of Public Affairs as the Director of Communications.*

# 11

# Markets in publicly-funded services – the case of demand-driven university funding

## Andrew Norton

Higher education in Australia is not a pure market. For domestic undergraduates, maximum fees, subsidies and soft loans all weaken price signals. These supports are unlikely to be abolished. Higher education is entrenched in the Australian model of the welfare state, with its widespread use of hybrid public-private funding and delivery of social services.

While higher education is not an economics textbook perfect market, its delivery can use market mechanisms. From 2012 to 2017 Australia experimented with a quasi-market 'demand-driven' funding system. Each university's funding moved from a bureaucratically fixed amount to one based on how many domestic bachelor's degree students they enrolled. The demand-driven system gave university and student choices a larger role in deciding who studied, what was studied, and where they studied.

Demand-driven funding ended for fiscal reasons in December 2017, but it attracted criticism on other grounds. Despite intellectual origins on the free market right, generally, pro-market people and organisations were among demand-driven funding's critics. They saw declining admission standards as a fault of demand-driven funding, along with the budget costs that led to its demise.

## The origins of demand-driven funding

Some institutions and practices on which demand-driven funding relied were in place long before it was introduced. Unlike public schools or vocational institutes, public universities were from their establishment independent of the government, legally and in most operational decisions. From 1974 universities were delegates of the Commonwealth government in deciding, through their admission processes, who received student subsidies and from 1989, when HECS was introduced, student loans. Prospective students already chose courses and universities through application systems designed to give them their highest-ranked preference. But the funding system was not organised to meet student demand. It allocated student places to universities, and sometimes also to fields of education or courses, based on historical, bureaucratic and political factors.

The idea that public funding systems could mimic markets in responding to demand owes much to the twentieth century's most influential free-market economist, Milton Friedman. He was an exponent of 'vouchers', using market mechanisms to allocate public funding.[16] Although the left continued to view markets with suspicion, and the right continued to view public funding with scepticism, vouchers neatly married two major streams of thought in Western politics. Voucher policies recognised the political inevitability, if not the desirability, of public funding, while using market mechanisms to create competition between producers and minimise the supply and demand mismatches of centralised resource allocation.

Originally vouchers for Australian higher education were proposed by the Liberal Party. They first appeared in a Liberal higher education policy in 1987, and reappeared in a more comprehensive form in the 1991 *Fightback!* package, and made it as far as the Howard Cabinet in 1999 (I worked on the Cabinet submission).[17] In 1987 the Liberal policy was for the government to award scholarships to students who could then take them to universities of their choosing. By 1999 the policy was to leave the government out of these decisions and to fund all accepted students – demand-driven funding is an uncapped voucher system. The 1990s Liberal voucher proposals combined them with market-set fees. This link between vouchers and deregulated fees was a political problem.

Demand-driven funding's political breakthrough was a 2008 review, commissioned by Julia Gillard as education minister and chaired by a former vice-chancellor, Denise Bradley.[18] Bradley's report recommended lifting bureaucratic controls on the number and distribution of student places. But she separated the questions of how to distribute student places and

16   Friedman & Friedman. 1962.
17   Norton. 2013.
18   Bradley, Noonan, Nugent, & Scales. 2008.

how to set fees. This removed the most contentious element of previous demand-driven funding proposals.

In 2009 Gillard accepted most of Bradley's recommendations. With Coalition support, funding caps were first relaxed and in 2012 abolished for bachelor's degree enrolments in public universities. While most attention focused on the lifting of funding ceilings, removing de facto funding floors was also important.[19] To maintain their enrolments and income universities faced new pressure to adapt what they offered to student preferences.

*Enrolment changes under demand-driven funding*

When demand-driven funding ended Australia's higher education system had evolved in ways a regulated system, with its focus on the political consequences of distributional decisions, could not have produced. Compared to overall enrolment growth between 2008 and 2017 of 38%, three universities more than doubled their enrolments and another eight grew by 50% or more. Some universities lost enrolment share, although none shrank below their 2008 absolute number of students.[20]

The demand-driven system also altered enrolment patterns between courses. Health-related courses expanded the most, reflecting the high demand for health workers and previously

---

19  Universities were penalised for 'under-enrolling' under the previous funding system. However, universities with weak first-preference demand were protected because the total number of student places in the system was held well below demand and their competitor universities had no financial incentive to expand enrolments significantly above their funding allocation.

20  Norton. 2020a.

unmet demand. Engineering enrolments grew with the mining boom, before dropping off after it ended. IT enrolments recorded above-average growth.[21] In these respects, the demand-driven system worked as planned.

Although the demand-driven system directed enrolments to areas of need, it also produced graduates who were, at least initially, surplus to professional labour market requirements. The end of the mining boom saw young adult professional employment decline, which combined with larger completing cohorts produced poor graduate employment outcomes.[22]

*Debates on the scale of enrolment*

The most persistent criticism of demand-driven funding was increased enrolments from less academically able students. Offers of student places to applicants with ATARs of 50 or below nearly quadrupled from less than 2,000 a year in 2010 to 7,620 in 2017 or nearly 7% of offers to applicants with an ATAR.[23] Other students admitted through pathway and mature age entry programs must have had original school results in the lower ATAR ranges since offers to high-ATAR school leavers were near-universal before demand-driven funding.[24] Selection requirements decline every time enrolments grow faster than population, as they did under demand-driven funding. *The Australian* newspaper and its columnists, usually sympathetic to market-based policies, regularly criticised this outcome.[25]

---

21  Ibid, p. 22.
22  Ibid., p .24.
23  DESE. 2020.
24  DEEWR. 2008.
25  Cater, 2014; Sloan, 2016; The Australian (editorial). 2013.

Concern about publicly-funded 'over-servicing' is not restricted to higher education. Medical student places are the most regulated part of the student funding system because the government fears that increasing the number of doctors, who like universities are delegated decision-makers on public funding, will lead to more unnecessary Medicare-funded consultations. In medicine, however, reasonably objective tests determine whether services are clinically justified. In higher education, disagreements about its role and purpose leave more space for contestable judgments about which applicants should be admitted and therefore funded.

If universities are understood as institutions of high-level intellectual inquiry then they should be restricted to the top 10 to 20% of the age cohort. ATARs are not completely reliable measures of academic ability, but this suggests an ATAR cut-off of around 80. If universities are understood as utilitarian suppliers of qualified workers, the perspective of the Morrison Government's Job-ready Graduates policy, the issue is less ATAR than the courses taken. Graduates in less vocational fields have relatively high rates of working in occupations unlikely to need their qualifications.[26]

While this utilitarian view combined with structural change in the economy is consistent with enrolment growth, it under-explains the long-term increase in higher education participation rates around the world.[27] Australia had already transitioned from an 'elite' to a 'mass' higher education system before demand-driven funding. From 30,000 students in 1950,

26    Norton, Cherastidtham, & Mackey. 2018b, chapter 10
27    Cantwell, Marginson, & Smolentseva. 2018.

the system reached nearly 600,000 government-supported students in 2008. Demand for higher education is driven by rising student and parent expectations and aspirations, which are often more general than aiming for a specific job.[28] Political pressure means that these expectations are eventually met under a wide variety of funding systems.

A mass higher education system accepts that there are many reasons why people want to go to university. Some universities may only cater to some of these reasons, but the higher education system as a whole is pluralistic. The task of student selection systems is not to enforce any one of these reasons but, so far as possible, to match students with appropriate courses and to minimise the risk of adverse outcomes.

## Selecting students

Perhaps surprisingly, until the demand-driven system university admissions were effectively unregulated. In 2012 a new national regulator, the Tertiary Education Quality and Standards Agency (TEQSA), was introduced. It regulates admissions standards that all higher education providers must meet. Initially, these required universities to check that applicants had 'adequate prior knowledge and skills to undertake the course of study successfully', later updating this to expressly mention academic preparation and require that there be 'no known limitations' to progress and completion.[29]

In thinking about how student selection works and could be

---

28   Norton. 2020c, 2020d.
29   This comes from various versions of the 'threshold standards', which are delegated legislation under the *Tertiary Education Quality and Standards Agency Act 2011*.

improved, we can turn to the twentieth century's second-most influential free-market thinker, Friedrich Hayek. So far as I am aware Hayek never wrote about university admissions, but his insights into the nature of knowledge are relevant. Even when we start with some broad principle of eligibility, such as 'adequate prior knowledge and skills, determining who fits the definition is often difficult.

Specific rules such as minimum ATARs, or the other academic criteria that could be used to uphold admission standards, hit problems with the imperfect nature of prior measures of academic ability, the complexity of assessing broader aptitude for a course, hidden and fluctuating levels of motivation, and little or no knowledge of other things going on in the applicant's life that might affect their chances of success. Although proxy indicators help predict success or failure, we are only ever talking about probabilities.[30]

How well a prospective student might do also depends on their course and university. Analysis of attrition rates shows that these differ, sometimes significantly, between universities after adjusting for a wide range of student and course characteristics known to affect levels of course non-completion.[31] Rather than setting general minimum admission standards, TEQSA's regulatory approach uses indicators such as attrition to assess potential breaches of admission standards, although it has never revealed what level of attrition triggers a regulatory response.[32]

---

30  Cherastidtham, Norton, & Mackey. 2018.
31  Ibid. p. 65; Higher Education Standards Panel. 2018.
32  TEQSA. 2019.

These processes reflect another Hayekian point, about markets as discovery mechanisms. Some of the knowledge needed for a good admissions decision can only be uncovered *after* the student starts, when all the different factors around the student's academic attributes, the student's broader life, their course and its teachers, and the wider university environment start interacting. Both sides of the transaction, the student and the university, learn from this experience.

## Improving student selection

A Grattan Institute report I co-authored in 2018 argued that critiques of higher education selection focus too much on a university's decision to admit.[33] Instead, a long process of mutual selection determines who is admitted to and retained in higher education. This process begins when ideas about future careers and post-school education start forming, officially starts with the student's application and the university's offer decision, then continues as applicants accept or reject offers, when students leave or stay at the census date when they incur student debt, remain or depart later in the first semester, and then pass or fail subjects.

Improved selection into universities and courses requires attention to all stages of this selection process, rather than expecting too much of university offer decisions. The Commonwealth and state governments have devoted more resources to career education, including a new National Careers Institute. My research shows that vocational education can

---

33   Norton, Cherastidtham, & Mackey. 2018a.

be a better option for lower-ATAR males (something already reflected in enrolments), as stereotypically male vocational occupations often pay more than the jobs lower-ATAR male graduates take.[34] Governments have promoted vocational education with advertising and free courses.

Census date management is also important to the mutual selection process. The census date is an unusual aspect of Australia's higher education system, giving most students a free 'try before you buy' period, typically for about a month, before any charge is incurred. In 2014, nearly 10% of students who accepted an offer never finalised their enrolment or ended it before the census date.[35] This is a large minority, but it should be larger. Many students do not understand the census date's significance and unnecessarily pay for subjects they never seriously engage with.[36] The census date's name should be changed to something like 'payment date' to highlight its consequences. In addition to better-protecting students, this would sharpen the incentive for universities to exercise care with their selection practices. Students who leave before the census date create costs but generate no revenue.

While mutual selection processes can be improved, trial and error is inevitable. Experience reveals information that nobody could have known before applications or offers. The expectation that both students and universities can get it right the first time is unrealistic. We do not expect this when purchasing other services, or when making other big life decisions on jobs and relationships.

---

34  Norton & Cherastidtham. 2019.
35  Norton et al. 2018a. p. 42.
36  Norton. 2020b. Stephenson, Cakitaki, & Luckman. 2021.

*Conclusion*

Higher education is an expensive publicly-funded service. It cannot be immune from fiscal constraints. Caps on university grants, imposed on Australian universities since 2018, are one way to achieve budget savings. Rules making people with low ATARs or other academic risk indicators ineligible for public support, as implied by criticisms of declining admission standards, are another.

But on Freidmanite and Hayekian grounds these approaches should be rejected. No neat empirical test shows which prospective student at the margins of suitability should be rejected and which accepted. Funding caps to exclude marginal students in practice affect students who are accepted by undermining the system's coordinating mechanisms. Popular courses and universities cannot expand because their funding is capped; their prospective students must take second or lower-preference courses or miss out on higher education.

Higher education savings should come from reduced per-student tuition subsidies and increased repayments of HELP loan scheme debt. This was what the government proposed in 2017 – the demand-driven system ended only as a second-best option when these alternative savings were rejected by the Senate. Students may not face strong price signals, but they are paying the price of this policy error.

*Andrew Norton is a Professor in the Practice of Higher Education Policy at the ANU Centre for Social Research and Methods.*

# 12

# Fixing housing policy

## Aaron Patrick

When John Howard lost his seat of Bennelong at the 2007 general election, free market advocates lost the contest to liberalise industrial relations. When Kevin Rudd was removed as Labor Party leader in 2010, attempts to tax resources more efficiently ended. Scott Morrison's defeat in 2022 killed a plan to allow some superannuation balances to be invested in property, a change that would have loosened funds' stranglehold over retirement savings.

Each event was a substantial setback for economic reform, with one substantial caveat. Morrison's superannuation policy was not responsible for the Coalition's election loss. The plan's brief existence – it was the official policy of the Australian Government for a week – was perceived within the Coalition as electorally popular. Some senior Liberal politicians have argued deploying it so late in the campaign was a timing mistake. Revealed earlier, it might have reduced the size of the Coalition's loss, they said. Others were concerned any longer exposure would have given time for a scare campaign by the superannuation industry to generate momentum.

Either way, the victory by an opposition that had promised little, if any, challenging policy changes sent a definitive message. Tax reform is dead. Industrial relations is lost. Energy markets are unlikely, for decades, to be freed. Government expansion looks inexorable, for now. The media has little interest in serious policy reform. The federal parliament is captured by interventionists. Even Coalition Treasury spokesman Angus Taylor, an economic conservative, doesn't advocate shrinking government.[37] Two decades into the new century, the cause of economic freedom in Australia has been lost. A prosperous but fearful nation has abandoned ambition.

So how should believers in the primacy of individual rights begin what will likely be a tortuous fight back? To make Australia a richer and more promising country for future generations? To convince Australians to trust themselves, rather than their governments? What's the tactical play?

Housing – the primary priority of almost every adult Australian – could provide economic liberals with a path back to relevance. Housing and property policy has been regarded by many experts as a reform sideshow.

After 20 years of failed attempts to improve the tax system, focusing on the mix of income, business and consumption taxes, a new approach is needed. Housing policy could be the starting point for a new generation of political leaders to advance economic reform.

---

37 Angus Taylor says government should shrink as a proportion of the economy but not in absolute terms.

The problem is obvious. The fix, although deeply difficult, is not unachievable. Success could invigorate liberalism. Housing is a route to fixing aged care, which is held back by the concentration of family wealth in housing. Solving the aged care problem could generate the political capital and policy credibility needed to expand and increase the GST, a pre-condition to cutting extravagant retirement welfare, which makes it impossible to lower personal income tax rates.

If personal taxes can become less punitive on the working classes – by which I mean anyone who relies on wages rather than capital or welfare to survive – business taxes could be cut. Significantly reducing corporate taxes as the culmination of a comprehensive free-market policy agenda could provide the greatest economic benefit to Australia since the great coal, gas and iron ore export boom at the start of this century. It could help unleash Australia's physical, intellectual and geographical potential, transforming the country into a place with the entrepreneurial drive of Silicon Valley, the wealth of Wall Street and the living standards of Singapore.

Economic, social and political reasons make housing a logical new starting point for the free-market project. Housing has become too expensive for many young individuals and families, even outside inner-city Sydney or Melbourne. At the start of the millennium, the average ratio of household debt to annual income was 67 times. By September 2022, it had reached 146 times. From Hobart to Broome, finding a pleasant dwelling that isn't expensive is hard.

Because of their family backgrounds, some Australians will never get the opportunity to enter the last remaining tax-favoured investment, property. Rising property prices make society richer, and more unequal. Expensive houses and apartments, relative to incomes, force non-wealthy people to live further away from jobs, make people poorer and exacerbate financial inequality. People with inheritances, which are untaxed, outbid the non-privileged, who rely on taxed income. The less fortunate are forced to the geographical fringes of society, or rental accommodation, or into debt that is harder for them to service.

That right-wing political parties should favour property owners' interests has long been a fixed position in Australia. Property-driven affluence was assumed to make voters more fiscally conservative.[38] This assumption was challenged by the election of a Labor Government in 2022, and the success of non-Liberal independent candidates in previously safe Liberal seats at that election and in 2019. The rise of 'teal' independents, who won eight seats in 2022 in what were previously Liberal electorates, has convinced many Liberal MPs and activists that the correlation between wealth and right-wing voting is fading.[39]

Homeownership may be a more important voting determinant than class or heading that way. The Australian Electoral Study, an in-depth survey of every election for the past 35 years, found

---

38  I wrongly predicted that property price gains would assist the Morrison Government at the 2022 election. By the time the election was held, capital city property prices had just started to fall. Some of the biggest drops would be in seats where independent candidates replaced Liberals, although any causal relationship is unclear. See: "Morrison's weapon is a $2.5 trillion payday," *The Australian Financial Review*. 14 January, 2022.

39  I classify Helen Haines in Victoria and Rebekha Sharkie from South Australia as teals, because their electorates were once held by the Liberal Party and they aren't obviously left wing, but not Andrew Wilkie, because his Hobart-based electorate would likely vote for the Labor and Greens party if he wasn't a candidate.

that 55% of people who voted for the Labor Party or Greens in 2022 were renters. 38% of homeowners voted for the Coalition. The Coalition-Labor spread is narrower when it comes to class. In the 2022 federal election, there were less than 10 percentage points between working-class support for Labor and the Coalition, down from a gap of more than 30 points in 1987.[40] A federal Liberal politician, Keith Wolahan, found the correlation between homeownership and Coalition voting stronger in his electorate of Menzies, one of only three Melbourne seats won by the Liberal Party. When two-party preferred swings were compared with 2021 census data showing home ownership, the correlation was clear and uniform. Areas with higher concentrations of renters were more likely to swing to the left. Looking beyond his electorate, he found that new apartment complexes the Victorian Government had approved next to train stations had high numbers of renters who were shifting some previously safe Liberal seats marginal.

The logical extension of Wolahan's analysis is that, as renting becomes even more popular, the electorate will permanently, if gradually, shift further left. This would be the continuation of a 50-year ownership trend. In 1971, 64% of 30 to 34-year-olds owned property. By 2021 the level was 50%, according to the Australian Institute of Health and Welfare.[41] For those aged 25 to 29, the rate fell from 50% to 36% over the same period. Among 50 to 54-year-olds age, the proportion fell from 80% to 72%.

To build new constituencies for his party, Wolahan suggested

40  Cameron, S. McAllister, I. Jackman, S, and Sheppard, J. 2022.
41  *Australian Institute of Health and* Welfare. 2022.

adopting policies that would help young, non or semi-professional couples buy into existing housing stock – to tip the scales their way when competing with investors. One of his suggestions was for the Liberal Party to review its support for unlimited negative gearing, which allows mortgage interest payments to be used as tax deductions. Wolahan said he understood the politics of the 2019 federal election, where the aspirations of teachers and tradies with one investment property featured in campaign rhetoric. But the tax rule, he said, favoured the "anesthetist with ten investment properties" who would more often than not outbid young couples looking to buy property for the first time.[42] Wolahan said that a younger population of propertyless Australians meant the political benefit exploited in 2019, when the Labor Party unsuccessfully proposed phasing out negative gearing, was now outweighed by a political cost.

Some economists have argued that negative gearing has little effect on housing prices. Peter Tulip, the Centre for Independent Studies' chief economist, has written that state and municipal-enforced housing restrictions, including tight zoning and minimum-size rules, are much bigger contributors to housing costs.[43]

Tulip calculated the average apartment in Sydney costs $500,000 to build, a figure that includes the builder's profit, land and financing costs. Limits on the availability of land and other rules raise the cost by $350,000 to $850,000. The 70% difference between the construction cost and the sale price is

42  Patrick, A. *Australian Financial Review*, 28 November, 2022.
43  Kendall, R, and Tulip, P. March, 2018.

usually captured by the owner of the land, or the developer, if the landowner doesn't appreciate the value of their asset, according to Tulip.

The analysis, which was taken up by Jason Falinski, a former Liberal Member for Mackellar in Sydney who chaired a parliamentary inquiry into house prices, pointed to two main conclusions. Regulation was the biggest cause of the cost of apartments, and it was enforced at the state and council levels. Falinski's committee's report recommended state governments abolish stamp duty, a tax on property sales, which essentially shifted responsibility for the problem to lower levels of government.[44]

Falinski's report analysed the problem rationally, not politically. There is a counterargument. Even if abolishing or restricting negative gearing has little effect on property prices, as a signature tax break, ending it would provide a potent signal of intent to aspiring home buyers.

Affluent municipalities appear more likely to oppose property development, including supermarkets that cater for middle and lower incomes. Some politicians, including Liberals, have exploited resistance to these developments for electoral purposes.[45] Ironically, though, most of the opposition to the construction of new housing, which could ameliorate economic inequality, has come from the left.

---

44  House of Representatives Standing Committee on Tax and Revenue. 2022.

45  In Sydney, Mosman Council's attempts to prevent a Woolworths outlet opening on the suburb's main road became a high-profile example in 2020 and 2021 of municipal opposition to development-based commerce. The council was led by a Liberal-aligned mayor. CHK See Patrick, A. "Mosman has a climate emergency, but no Woolworths," *The Australian Financial Review*, 11 December, 2020.

In Sydney's Leichhardt suburb the mayor, Jamie Parker, led the opposition in 2010 to the construction of 1250 apartments that would replace a disused trotting track. Parker predicted the development would trigger a fall in nearby property prices and a large increase in traffic.

Known as Forrest Lodge, the district was transformed. Between the censuses of 2011 and 2016 the share of high-rise apartments in the area rose from 10% of dwellings to 46%. It was one of the largest shifts of its type seen in Sydney. Prices in the adjoining suburbs of Annadale, Camperdown and Glebe kept rising, increasing the wealth of already-prosperous residents. Parker, a Member of the Greens party, was elected to the New South Wales Parliament in 2011. He continued to oppose new housing in the area, including on the site of a disused power plant known as White Bay, until his retirement in 2023.

The Forrest Lodge example demonstrates two important dynamics of the housing policy debate: playing to residents' prejudices can be an effective tactic for individual politicians; the arguments employed are often selfish and dishonest.

The central problem with making housing more affordable is that it may be difficult to achieve without hurting the financial interests of existing owners, who comprise more than half the population. Tulip has advocated for the construction of 1 million new dwellings, which he estimates would lower property prices and rents by 25%.[46] A shift of this magnitude would reduce Australians' collective wealth by approximately $250 billion.

---

46  Tulip, P. 27 October, 2022.

In this store of wealth lies the political and economic challenge of making housing cheaper. Retirees and pensioners – the greatest beneficiaries of long-term property price rises - are an important and powerful constituency for right-wing political parties. With plenty of time to worry about their finances, retirees are a politically engaged group.

About 70% of those over-65 receive welfare. As Australia ages – about 25% of us will be over 65 by 2047 – it is only fair on younger generations that the elderly cover most of the cost of their retirements. Which in many cases would mean cashing in their homes, a step the Morrison Government tentatively encouraged in its 2021 budget by expanding a little-used reverse-mortgage scheme.[47]

The taxation system encourages couples to remain in large homes long after their children have left home. Their property is shielded from capital gains tax and the wealth cut-off for the age pension. Good-quality apartments located near their houses and social networks would provide an incentive for retirees to switch to apartments. Their former houses could be sold to young families with children or converted into apartments.

Eventually, it should become seen as selfish for retired couples and singles to live in multi-bedroom houses. Society should come to regard these houses as precious resources that should be available to families. Such a shift in attitude would make it politically easier to end or reduce the incentives provided by the taxation system for couples or individuals to live in large houses.

---

47   Kehoe, J. 12 May, 2021.

As for the young, potential beneficiaries, they need to be convinced that free-market policies can help them achieve the financial security offered by home ownership. Young Australians don't trust the right. After the 2022 election, federal Liberal Party director Andrew Hirst told Liberal MPs that his research had found 67% of voters believed the party "had fallen behind the views of modern Australia".[48]

The Liberal Party's inability to attract young Australians could pose a long-term threat to its existence. Young Australians perceive themselves as more committed to social tolerance than their parents. Questions of personal identity have become more important. Just as the threat of nuclear war overshadowed the lives of young people growing up in the 1980s, global warming is of deep and genuine concern for young people today. They regard sexual identity as more fluid than older generations. They see institutional racial bias where older people don't. These perception shifts pose a profound threat to the future of the Liberal Party.

The Liberal Party is losing the centre. It is conceivable that the centrist independents will morph into a party that represents the affluent middle classes. If the Liberal Party abandoned or lost hope in wealthy inner suburbs, and retreated to the more conservative outer suburbs, it would likely be taken over by the Queensland Liberal National Party and conservative elements in other states. A new, populist party could emerge similar to France's National Rally, Israel's Lukid or Northern Ireland's Democratic Unionist Party. These parties, led by dominant individual leaders for most of their existence, have limited

---

48   Patrick, A. 30 September, 2022.

internal contests over ideology. They are not parties of broad coalitions.

The consequence of an ideologically narrower Liberal Party would likely be semi-permanent minority status in the federal parliament. Periods in government would come from ad hoc coalitions with the Nationals, which might split into conservative and non-conservative rural-based parties, and independents or smaller parties.

There is a natural tendency, at any moment, to expect the future will repeat the past. Particularly in political parties with long histories of power, there is a belief in a cycle that makes returns to government inevitable. This confidence is mistaken. There is no guarantee that parties like the Liberals will be able to keep up with the changes happening in Australia or preserve the internal coalition of conservative and liberal wings crucial to the success of any broad-based party. Believers in free markets, to influence government, need to build a constituency for liberalism. Power will not be handed to them. Nor should it.

*Aaron Patrick is a senior correspondent at the Australia Financial Review.*

# 13

# Reforming the states

# Chris Rath

Few today would disagree that Australia's golden era of economic reform was from 1983 to 2007. This 'longest decade of reform', as described by George Megalogenis, saw privatisation, deregulation, tariff protection slashed, a new modern tax system, and a more flexible labour market. Productivity growth was the preeminent objective and free enterprise was celebrated rather than demonised. The Hawke-Keating Labor Government and the Howard-Costello Liberal Government that replaced it seemed to be more of a continuation of each other rather than a repudiation, at least in terms of economic policy. This reform nirvana, unfortunately, ended with the election of Rudd and the global financial crisis that hit early in his term. The subsequent period of 2007 to 2023 could be categorised as 'the longest decade of inaction on economic reform', from both sides of the political divide.

But why is it that we only ever view economic reform as the remit of the federal government? State governments after all have huge expenditures and balance sheets. They have vast state-owned enterprises and are primarily responsible for most of the services and infrastructure we rely upon. And Australia's most inefficient taxes are levied at a state level, from payroll tax and stamp duty to insurance taxes and the emergency services levy. State economic reform is often the missing piece of the puzzle, and when done well - like has so frequently been the case in New South Wales since 2011 - goes mostly unnoticed. Of course, that is both a blessing, as state legislators can quietly go about reform without the heightened attention presented to our federal counterparts, and a curse, as important state economic reforms rarely get the credit they deserve.

The New South Wales economy is far more dynamic and successful today because of twelve years of Liberal Government reforms. Yet, there is still so much more that could be done at a state level, with four major reforms I believe are worthy of consideration.

*Phasing out payroll tax*

Any serious attempt at economic reform must consider the tax system, especially at the state level since that is where so many of Australia's most inefficient taxes are levied. Particular attention must be paid to taxes placed upon private enterprise, as such taxes directly affect employment outcomes and wealth creation. It has long been understood that, although the legal incidence of a tax on business lies with employers, the real financial burden of poorly designed taxes eventually shifts along the market, either to employees or consumers. The most notorious example of this effect is observed in payroll tax.

Payroll tax is the largest state and territory-levied tax, providing governments with $24.7 billion in revenue in 2020-21[49], representing nearly a third of all tax revenue raised. Australia is one of the few countries within the OECD that levies a payroll tax. In theory, payroll tax is efficiently levied on the capital of medium and large-sized employers when the total taxable wages paid to their employees exceeds a threshold amount, in New South Wales that amount is $1.2 million (2022/23). However, in reality, the 2010 Henry Tax Review identified payroll tax as the third most inefficient tax country-wide, primarily stemming from each state or territory's distortionary tax threshold, multi-category exemptions, and differing regulatory interpretations.[50]

The payroll tax threshold creates a market distortion where, for small business owners with wages payable hovering around the threshold amount, it is more profitable to remain inefficiently small than to expand business operations to match the true market equilibrium. As a result, the potential deadweight loss is often counterbalanced by businesses passing on the cost of their payroll tax liability either to employees (through a reduction in labour costs, wages and/or headcount) or to consumers (through increased prices or lower quality). Payroll tax might not be a 'tax on jobs' by intention, but it certainly has become so by effect, most particularly for those small and medium businesses looking to expand beyond the threshold.

The New South Wales Productivity Commission has identified on multiple occasions[51] that discordant rates, exemptions,

49    Australian Bureau of Statistics. 2023.
50    Commonwealth of Australia. 2010.
51    New South Wales Treasury. 2018.

and reporting obligations between jurisdictions also impede businesses attempting to expand inter-state. These differences serve as additional red tape, both for the government in managing revenue collection and for employers looking to hire across state boundaries. Increased costs to consumers created by payroll tax's distortionary threshold, lower employee wages, and incongruence between jurisdictions, among other inefficiencies, are estimated to cause more than 40 cents of economic damage for each dollar of additional revenue raised.[52]

Given payroll tax's offence to market efficiency across Australia, the New South Wales Government should be commended for recently increasing the payroll tax threshold and reducing the payroll tax rate, especially during the pandemic budgets of 2020/21 and 2021/22. However, ultimately payroll tax must either be replaced or eliminated. Replacement would require a unified state-federal reform approach. The rationale is outlined in recommendation 57 of the Henry Tax Review affirming that "State payroll taxes should eventually be replaced with revenue from more efficient broad-based taxes that capture the value-add of labour". A common proposal in this line of thought involves the federal government broadening the base of the Goods and Services Tax (GST) and increasing the rate, exchanging each state or territory's payroll tax income for federal contributions from the new and expanded GST. This replacement approach no doubt seems like an elegant solution, however, getting such an agreement across nine state, federal and territory jurisdictions of all political persuasions and economic circumstances would be a formidable task.

---

52   ACCI. 2014.

In contrast to 'replacement', it is indeed possible to eliminate payroll tax without the need for federal cooperation. To do so would require a bold plan to gradually phase out payroll tax over time. The tax would be eliminated incrementally with slight reductions in the rate every year for 20 years. The small shortfalls in revenue each year would be covered by the natural annual increases in revenue of all other taxation sources. After 20 years, payroll tax would be eliminated, and overall revenue would still be higher in 2043 than in 2023. There would be no requirement to cut spending in each state or territory budget. The only caveat is that state and territory governments would be forced to restrain their expenditure to only modest increases, in line with Treasury forecasts.

Neither replacement nor elimination of payroll tax would be easy to achieve politically, but the economic benefits would be enormous. It's not solely about removing deadweight loss in the tax system as a concept, but also about encouraging businesses to grow and the greater employment opportunities that follow. In particular, any state that moves first on the elimination approach would attract new business investment and employment from other higher-taxing state jurisdictions. New South Wales should act unilaterally and become the beneficiary.

*Phasing out stamp duty*

Like payroll tax, the 2010 Henry Tax Review identified state-based stamp duties on property (sometimes called transfer duty or conveyance stamp duty) as among the most inefficient taxes in Australia. Stamp duty is a significant source of state revenue despite being volatile, inequitable, inefficient, and inconsistent with the needs of a modern tax system. It is a volatile form of revenue because it is subject to Australia's ever-changing property prices and, more particularly, the highly fluctuating quantum of property transactions. It is inequitable as people who move more frequently pay more tax, irrespective of their income or wealth. And it is inefficient and outdated because the tax's high deadweight loss is created from discouraging transactions, meaning property misallocation away from its most valuable use.

As practical examples, this infamously productivity-stifling tax means that first home buyers face a huge barrier to entering the market; those aiming to upsize to suit their family needs are inhibited from moving; elderly Australians are remaining in their oversized homes for longer than is necessary; investors find their assets even more illiquid as they hang on to their properties longer to recoup the cost of stamp duty; and labour is inefficiently allocated to housing as people are less likely to move to change jobs or their location of employment.

The need for stamp duty reform is clear. What is ultimately required is the replacement of stamp duty in the form of a land tax, which is overall far less inefficient and more revenue stable. An annual land tax would consist of a fixed amount plus a rate applied to the (improved or unimproved) land value of a property. Crucially, state and territory governments would be required to commit to a locked indexation, ensuring land tax rates will not disproportionately increase over time. Treasury studies in New South Wales have indicated that a land tax model would result in a 3-4% reduction in home prices, whilst at the same time enabling a forecast 1.7% increase to gross state product from productivity increases.[53]

The question then arises: how will state and territory governments account for the initial shortfall in revenue from the transition to land tax? One option is federal assistance in recouping losses through temporarily increasing other more efficient taxes, such as the GST. However, in much the same way as payroll tax, federation-wide tax reform is near impossible as it requires reaching an agreement across nine state, federal and territory jurisdictions of all political persuasions and economic circumstances. My preference is for New South Wakes to act unilaterally rather than wait impatiently for a federal solution.

Unilateral action is possible, and the Australian Capital Territory Labor Government should be congratulated for first initiating stamp duty reform more than a decade ago. Most first-home buyers in the Australian Capital Territory are today completely exempt from paying stamp duty if the property costs less than $1 million, and by 2032 there will be no duty on property transfers in the territory at all. Similarly, the New South Wales Liberal Government has started this reform by giving first-home buyers a choice between stamp duty and a small annual land tax on purchases under $1.5 million. The New South Wales Government should expand this scheme to include all owner-occupied properties on future purchases under $1.5 million, with the threshold increasing by $50,000 every year in perpetuity. In the long run, a transition to land tax is revenue neutral, however, expanding the scheme will mean budget gaps in the short term. Limiting the reform to only owner-occupied properties and including a threshold

---

53   New South Wales Property Tax Proposal. 2021.

will ensure that those budget gaps are more manageable than under an immediate total abolition scenario. But also, by slowly increasing the threshold each year, more properties will become eligible, meaning eventually stamp duty is phased out entirely.

The New South Wales Government's first tranche of the reforms, pertaining to first home buyers alone, simply absorbed the budget shortfalls out of consolidated revenue. An expanded or second tranche would ideally be funded by reducing government expenditure (as outlined in Part III). However, if the government was not inclined to reduce spending to fund the reforms, and federal assistance was not an option, then thought should be given to a temporary increase in council rates as a short-term replacement source of revenue collected by the state government. Council rates are outlined as one of the most efficient forms of taxation in the Henry Tax Review, due to the immobility of land. Nonetheless, a temporary rate increase should be considered as a last resort, with federal tax replacement like GST, consolidated revenue, and expenditure reductions all being preferable. Like all impactful reforms, phasing out stamp duty requires political willpower, and while New South Wales is on the right track with first-home buyers, it should be viewed as only the beginning of a much longer process of reform.

## Refocusing and Restraining Expenditure

Accompanying bold plans to reform payroll tax and stamp duty, it is necessary to go 'back to basics' briefly to review government expenditure. Minimising unnecessary expenditure is an economic imperative for any government that seeks to manage taxpayer money responsibly. Sensible expenditure constraints lead to greater value per-dollar for taxpayers and a reduction in overall debt and deficit. I am principally advancing two approaches to managing expenditure: refocusing budget announcements to be outcomes-focused and ending the practice of pork barrelling.

There exists fundamentally flawed thinking that more and more government spending will lead to better outcomes in health, education, transport or other services. Most budget accomplishments are defined by volumes of expenditure – 'record' and 'unprecedented' funding – whose material outcomes are difficult to ascertain. Whilst volumes of spending aren't inherently bad indicators of a government's priorities, justification for new expenditure should instead be made based on foreseeable outcomes, as opposed to abstruse dollar figures. Ronald Reagan once remarked that the "government does not tax to get the money it needs; government always finds a need for the money it gets", pointing to the large wastage associated with public spending.

A shift is therefore needed in our approach to government projects, from being input-focused (talking in dollar figures) to outcome-focused (talking in statistical outcomes and results). An idea that aligns with this concept of outcome-focused spending is to implement key performance indicators for how taxpayer money is spent by the government, tied to statistics from sources such as the ABS or the relevant state treasury. For example, what was once a "$300 million local hospital upgrade" now becomes "an initiative to cut local hospital waiting times by one hour".

An even better solution would be to enable individuals themselves to choose how their taxpayer funds are spent through the delegation of responsibility for certain kinds of expenditure. One of the best, but most politically daring, examples is the idea of school vouchers, where parents issue a certificate of funding to the school that they decide is most appropriate for their child - public or private – thereby providing choice and competition in education. Choice in schooling then becomes available to everyone, not just the wealthy, through government funding and a competitive market. Where there is choice, greater efficiency is the result.

The second substantial treasury reform is the need to crack down on pork-barrelling, a practice at every level of government that should be offensive to all political persuasions. Pork-barrelling is both immoral and inefficient, creating scenarios where genuine community need is overlooked by the government in favour of funding more politically advantageous projects. Elected officials and not bureaucrats should determine how taxpayer funds are spent, but it should be transparent, and the funding should only be limited to core services. Transparency means that grants and funding proposals should have their business cases independently scrutinised and benefit-cost ratios determined. For major projects, above a certain threshold, credible independent organisations like the Productivity Commission could be used. Any Minister that deviates from the independent advice or ignores the benefit-cost ratios must publicly disclose their reasons for doing so.

Pork-barrelling can also be curbed by ensuring that the government only focuses on core services and infrastructure. At the 2022 federal election, we saw outrageous profligacy from the Morrison Government, with announcements such as $10 million for regional newspapers and $15 million for breweries. These grants are not the core function of government, as important as those businesses may be. Pork-barrelling in this manner could be avoided by reducing the amount of money the government has available for such projects. The government should be forced to adhere to prudent budget principles. For example, expenses growth should be capped at 2% and should not be allowed to exceed revenue growth. Furthermore, the government must always maintain a AAA credit rating from all rating agencies and should never hand down a deficit over 1% of GDP, with a surplus and no net debt always being the aim. This reduces the pool of funds available for new and unnecessary projects that are so often at the heart of pork-barrelling and heeds the advice of Peter Costello that "the easiest cut you will make is the stuff you never go into".

Reducing the quantum of taxpayer money available for pork-barrelling by imposing an expenditure growth cap of 2% per year also fits well with the elimination of payroll tax policy detailed above. Governments cannot afford huge spending sprees if revenue growth is constrained due to gradual payroll tax reductions over two decades.

No doubt governments of all persuasion enjoy the benefits of new spending announcements for political gain. But I seriously question the political benefit of pork-barrelling in an increasingly well-informed and sceptical electorate that values integrity and could consider politicians brandishing novelty-size cheques as an attempt to buy their vote. Governments are the custodians of taxpayers' funds, and we should only spend their money with an abundance of caution and care.

## Privatisation

Beyond structural reform, treasuries Australia-wide have options to privatise portions of their assets to raise funds for infrastructure projects, healthcare and schools. Privatised assets that exist within a competitive market or are properly regulated, such as QANTAS or 49% of the New South Wales electricity grid, have proven historically successful in raising capital for other significant investments. Privatisation also provides an incentive for innovation and greater efficiency in fields previously the sole domain of government.

New South Wales has been a huge beneficiary of privatisation over the last 12 years. We call it 'asset recycling' not for political branding but instead for accuracy, as the capital unlocked from selling or leasing one asset is then invested into building another, until that new asset is built and the capital once again unlocked to build another, and so the cycle continues. It allows governments to build new productive infrastructure like major road and rail projects without plunging into huge debt.

The 2016-17 electricity network transaction was the state's most notable example of asset recycling. By leasing 49% of the state's 'poles and wires' over a 99-year horizon, the state's coffers generated net proceeds of $23 billion, exceeding expectations by about $2 billion Profits raised from the transaction funded the Rebuilding v infrastructure program which included a budget for public transport, new roads, new schools, new health facilities, upgraded cultural attractions, and water security improvements.

The Productivity Commission in 2013 recommended that state-owned electricity networks be privatised as they are less efficient than their private sector peers.[54] This is hardly surprising, as state-owned enterprises are not subject to the price mechanism and the forces of supply and demand. In many ways, privatisation is an easy version of economic reform. Instead of Treasury officials painstakingly trying to force inefficient government monopolies to become more dynamic, that job is outsourced to the private sector, led by shareholder and customer expectations.

The New South Wales Government should consider leasing its remaining 51% share of the state's electricity network – 100% of Essential Energy and 49.6% of Ausgrid and Endeavour Energy – to drive efficiency and to receive a revenue boost akin to that of 2016-17.[55] The 'recycled' revenue from the new lease would provide an opportunity to invest in even more infrastructure to boost the state's productivity, supporting and expanding upon current plans such as the Western Harbour Tunnel and Beaches Link, Sydney Metro, Circular Quay Precinct Renewal, Parramatta Light Rail Stage 2, and new school and hospital upgrades. Other state and territory governments would benefit from simultaneously adopting analogous privatisation measures.

Whether it be privatisation, tax reform or expenditure restraint, there is no doubt that state governments are ripe for bold economic reform. Too often these important reforms are

---

54   Productivity Commission. 2013.
55   New South Wales Treasury. 2017.

kicked down the road on the basis that federal assistance is needed or an inability to get an agreement among jurisdictions. This is mostly a cop-out and shows a complete lack of creative thinking and tenacity. Federation-wide economic reform is always preferable, but I have outlined that four major reforms could be achieved unilaterally, and of course, there would be many more. Increasing the housing supply and reforming the New South Wales planning system is a critical reform area to improve housing affordability and grow the state's economy. Deregulation and reducing red tape on businesses, large and small, is often spoken about but rarely actioned. Competition policy, industrial relations, and the efficiency of the public service require critical reform. And of course, if tough conversations need to take place with the federation, they should start by addressing vertical fiscal imbalance and horizontal fiscal equalisation. New South Wales should be celebrated as a bastion of economic reform over the last 12 years. But further productivity-enhancing reforms are required for our continued prosperity, especially now during trying times. What is ultimately required is for us to seize the initiative and create our own longest decade of economic reform; such reforms require ingenuity and courage from our state's political leaders if they are to succeed.

*Chris Rath is a Member of the Legislative Council in the Parliament of New South Wales. Before that he worked in the insurance industry.*

# 14

# A country with less regulation will have a smaller government

## Gerard Rennick

The term 'free market' is in many ways an oxymoron. There are very few markets that aren't regulated by one of Australia's three levels of government.

The aim of regulators should therefore be to regulate fairly and efficiently to maximise productivity whilst minimising regulation. A fair market will scorn subsidies. An efficient market will scorn unnecessary regulation.

There are only two outcomes in a market, you're either making money or losing money. Profitability, measured as return on equity is the benchmark by which markets should be measured.

Capitalism and the risk-reward paradigm that drives it are what will maximise productivity. When making regulations governments should seek to promote and protect capitalism. Capitalism can be defined as the process where people risk their capital. This is defined in a broad sense as the labour of a carpenter or mechanic, the mind of a scientist or engineer, the heart of a teacher or nurse or the persistence and perseverance of business owners.

From a political perspective, the ideological view of the world through the political prism of left verse right is a false dichotomy. Instead, the world should be seen through the prism of the entity that risks its capital verse the entity that seeks to either regulate or manage other people's capital.

The further removed the management class is from the capital they risk, the greater the chance for sub-optimal outcomes. This idea is understood in economics as agency theory.

When one reviews Australia's economy and society over the last 50 years individual risk-taking, productivity and personal responsibility have been scorned in favour of government intervention and consumption. On the other hand, the provision of essential services, many of them monopolies, has been outsourced to an unaccountable managerial or bureaucratic class that owns none of the capital they manage.

In summary, Australia has pursued the opposite of capitalism in favour of a hybrid socialist-neoliberal economy where risk-takers are punished and rent seekers are rewarded. This has seen the rise of a bureaucratic mandarin class that is regulating Australia into servitude. It has also seen the rise of an unaccountable corporate sector that has gained control of sovereign industries and leveraged their strategic importance for rent-seeking purposes.

This has resulted in the decline of Australia's productive capacity, especially its manufacturing and energy sector, to the point where Australia is no longer self-reliant in many strategic sovereign industries. As illustrated by the impact on Germany of the war in Ukraine, the provision of energy has national security implications. Such an essential and strategic service cannot be left in hands of those more interested in short-term profits, driven by scalping distortions in market rules that divide the provision of energy into five-minute blocks.

If Australia is to regain its true independence and provide our children, the chance for a prosperous future many government policies implemented over the last 50 years need to be abolished. During this time Australia has succumbed to a dangerous mixture of neo-Marxism (think identity politics) and neo-liberalism (think privatisation by virtual signalling rent seekers espousing aforementioned identity politics).

The government does play an important role in democratic societies. However, their role should be restricted to the role of essential services that an individual can't take responsibility for. For example, while an individual should be responsible for their health in terms of eating well and exercising, they cannot build a hospital. An individual can restrict their power usage but can't build a power station.

There is any number of reforms governments should address to reduce the size of the government and liberate the market players from the burden of excessive regulation. A few major reforms are outlined below.

The priority of 'free market' reform should be the abolition of superannuation. It is a rent seeker's paradise that generates nothing other than fees for paper shufflers. It transfers wealth from the active worker to the passive manager who has no risk exposure whatsoever. It is both a productivity and entrepreneurial killer.

After 30 years, superannuation has failed to reduce the number of people on the pension by a significant amount. Around 70% of retirees are still on a full or part pension. The tax concessions alone cost the Federal budget $50 billion annually, most of which accrues to the upper 20% of income earners. The pension costs $53 billion for the lower 70% of income earners.

The 2021 retirement income review estimated that superannuation tax concessions will soon exceed the cost of the pension. In terms of protecting the federal budget from a blowout in pension costs, superannuation is not fit for purpose.

Superannuation administration costs are estimated to be at least $30 billion per year. This is a cost to the economy that yields no genuine outcomes. That sort of capital should be invested in productive industries such as infrastructure and manufacturing. Instead, it is a massive subsidy to the financial services industry.

There is a hidden agency cost to superannuation. Union-dominated industry funds now control over 20% of many of Australia's blue-chip corporations. This gives unions enormous power in corporate boardrooms, the result of which has seen Australia's industries become driven by ideology rather than productivity. It has also seen market pricing driven by capital inflows rather than profitability.

Coalition Governments have stood idly by while unions generate rivers of gold from superannuation fees.

The Keating Government never sought a mandate from the people asking if their hard-earned dollars should be handed over to unaccountable managers with no capital guarantee. This is not surprising. Had a mandate for compulsory superannuation been put to the people, the answer would have been a resounding no. New Zealanders were asked what they thought of compulsory superannuation in a 1997 referendum. They voted a resounding 92% to 8% against it.

In terms of 'free market' ideology, there is nothing free about superannuation. It is a mandated gravy train that is more akin to communism than capitalism.

Taxation is another area that desperately needs reform. Australian tax laws are littered with loopholes and exemptions that favour passive investment at the expense of active productivity. Australia's tax laws also encourage profits earned onshore to be sent offshore.

Taxation reforms should include capital gains being taxed at the same rate as active income. All CGT concessions on all assets should be removed. A CGT-free threshold for the principal place of residence could be maintained.

Tax concessions for offshore investors should also be abolished. The rate of tax on profits transferred offshore should not be lower that the corporate tax rate for profits retained in Australia. Politicians should focus on retaining profits derived in Australia as a means of retaining capital rather than attracting more foreign debt.

CGT concessions have caused house prices to climb to levels outside the reach of younger generations. The average price of a house in Australia is estimated to be over ten times the average earnings whereas forty years ago it was four times the average. High asset values are destroying the aspirations of our younger generations.

The Coalition should heed the rise of the Greens and Teals in the recent election. It is not just environmental issues driving younger people to vote for these parties. Their mantra of taxing the rich gains more traction the higher house prices go.

There is too much capital invested in the housing sector at the expense of more productive industries. Taxes need to be flatter and encourage greater productivity rather than speculation or consumption.

There is no better example of the failure of neo-liberal economics than the energy market. Privatisation of essential services with national security implications has been a disaster that has impacted not just the energy market, but downstream industries that rely on cheap and reliable energy to remain viable and competitive on global markets.

Essential service monopolies with sovereign characteristics should never be held to ransom by virtue signalling rent seekers. Many of these rent seekers speak out of both sides of their mouths. On the one hand, they espouse free market economics while pocketing government subsidies courtesy of the taxpayer.

It's probably fair to argue the privatisation of fast-moving retail services companies like Telstra and Qantas has been successful. On the other hand, it is questionable if the same can be said for energy markets.

The baseload energy market should be nationalised and subsidies for renewable energy cease. Those organisations who wish to compete in the energy market are more than welcome to do so by providing a full array of energy services not just limited to generation, but also transmission, storage, security, and recycling services.

If the ideologues are correct and the private sector is more efficient, it shouldn't be too difficult for private sector operators to undercut the national baseload energy market in price and reliability without subsidies.

The supply of energy from the private sector should not be bought in 15-minute blocks but as yearly contracts. Service level agreements should place the risk on the provider to ensure the provision of reliable energy rather than the government having to underwrite reliability.

Nuclear and hydropower should become a larger part of Australia's energy mix. There is an abundance of uranium and hydroelectric sites in Australia. The Barakula State Forest in Southern Queensland is the largest in the Southern Hemisphere. Straddled on the edge of the Darling Downs it perfectly triangulates Southeast and Central Queensland and is the perfect location for a nuclear power plant. The power plant could easily connect to the southern interconnector at the nearby Kogan Creek power plant as well as provide cheap energy for industries wishing to capitalise on the nearby proposed inland railway line to Gladstone and Nathan Dam site.

Nuclear and Hydro energy can provide other sovereign

capabilities in areas such as defence, agriculture, water security, tourism, and the environment.

Institutionalised childcare is one of Australia's fastest-growing industries. Despite increased government subsidies from $500 million to $10 billion in two decades, institutionalised childcare has not seen an improvement in Australia's education rankings.

It has however caused a massive increase in the size of United Voice, Australia's fastest-growing union. Most of the 150,000 childcare workers are unionised and as such, it is estimated that they contribute close to $100 million to the union movement in membership fees.

Governments should not be involved in co-parenting children. Forcing parents to select institutionalised childcare if they are to receive any sort of childcare assistance is an affront to the concept of Australia as a free democratic country and to family values.

Childcare, to the extent that it is paid, should be paid directly to parents (except where social welfare is an issue) so they can choose the best form of childcare for their family. Many parents work shift hours. These include nurses, police, transport, and hospitality workers. They cannot use childcare services. Many parents may prefer to use nannies, their parents or even stay home themselves, especially those on lower incomes.

One of the great paradoxes of the move to bigger government is that the Liberal party has embraced it. Big government and rent-seeking behaviour should be anathema to a party that espouses small government and reward for effort. The failure to stand up for its values will haunt the credibility of the Liberal party in the future.

On a macro level, productivity in Australia is severely curtailed by nine governments that serve a population of just 26 million people

Australia's federation needs a drastic overhaul. Of all Australia's problems, none is greater that the vertical fiscal imbalance and ambiguous responsibilities between the federal and state governments. A constitutional convention or something of a similar ilk is desperately needed to resolve these issues.

There is no greater rent seeker in the country than state governments. This is just as much the fault of the federal government as it is of state governments. The blame game between the two levels of government needs to end.

Serious thought should be given to whether three levels of government are needed in Australia. Would it not be better to empower local regional communities with their own policing, health, and education?

State taxes should also be reformed. Most discussion around reforming state taxes focuses on abolishing stamp duty. In my view, it is not stamp duty which is a tax on speculation that should be abolished but rather payroll tax. Taxing employers to employ people is a productivity killer and makes it harder for Australian industry to compete in global markets. Stamp duty on share trading could be re-introduced to fund the abolition of payroll tax. Share trading, like superannuation administration, doesn't produce any goods or services.

Regardless of the reforms proposed, the duplication of

responsibilities between tiers of government needs to stop. Australia would have to be one of the most over-governed counties on earth. It has been alleged that government spending as a proportion of GDP is higher in Australia than it is in China. Is it a wonder that Australia's industries are struggling to compete with the rest of the world?

The least understood responsibility when it comes to markets and government responsibility is monetary policy. As a sovereign country, Australia should control not just the price of its currency but the volume of currency. This is not a new concept. Governor Macquarie adopted this method with the introduction of the holey dollar, Australia's first currency in 1810. It was also a recommendation of the 1937 Royal commission into banking.

If you think the sale of sovereign infrastructure to offshore interests is bad, it is nothing compared to the outsourcing of Australia's printing press.

The biggest market in the world is the United States Treasury Bond market. It is controlled by the United States Federal Reserve whose ownership structure remains opaque.

While Australia has the privilege of borrowing in AUD, the money loaned to it is ultimately through intermediaries that source their funding from the major central banks via currency swaps, predominately the United States Federal Reserve.

For some strange reason, the RBA has outsourced control over the volume of credit in Australia to foreign central banks. I believe that this has cost Australia billions if not trillions in foregone wealth.

For example, if the Australian Government builds a dam at a cost of a billion dollars, and funds it via foreign debt, the first billion dollars in wealth created must repay that foreign debt. Interest on the loan is also paid offshore. That means Australia has just given up over a billion dollars in wealth because the government outsourced its sovereign capacity to fund itself to a group of unelected and unaccountable foreign bankers.

The rules around the RBA funding Australian governments are simple. The debt can only be issued if it is secured against nation-building infrastructure that generates a return for the government. This would include dams, power stations, airports, ports, telecommunications, and toll roads.

This is not a radical concept. Private entities use secured lending to fund investments all the time. Why Australian governments pay private financiers at the expense of the taxpayers can only be put down to blind ignorance in understanding how monetary policy works.

The use of the quantitative easing lever is not just a cost-saving measure. It provides another lever in managing the economy. The current outbreak of inflation is a good example. While I believe that interest rates should be raised gradually over time, raising them too quickly, as the RBA is currently doing will only damage the economy.

Rather than damage the economy through austerity measures, the RBA should increase supply by increasing productivity. Building more power stations, dams and other infrastructure will drive down the price of power, water, and other services to make the cost of living and doing business cheaper.

While these measures will take time to implement, they are much more productive than changing the price of money monthly that only rewards speculators rather than producers.

Unfortunately, the RBA did print money during the Covid crisis, but this measure damaged the economy rather than grew it as the money was used for consumption rather than investment.

Governments need to get back to providing services rather than regulating every aspect of people's lives. They need to empower the individual rather than enslave them through government dependence. This means people take responsibility for their health, their retirement, and their children. This is the role of the family and the community, not the government. Government should then focus on ensuring the taxes they collect are used to provide essential services efficiently and fairly.

*Gerard Rennick is a Senator representing Queensland in the Parliament of Australia. Before that he worked in financial services.*

# 15

# Markets and prosperity

## By Harry Stutchbury

Free trade and globalisation have hollowed out the middle class of developed western countries, suppressing wages and living standards below those experienced before these two forces reshaped economies. Re-patriating key industries, particularly in manufacturing, will reverse this trend and reinvigorate our economies while buttressing them from future COVID-like shocks.

Or so goes the narrative driven by the political left and, more recently, the populist right emboldened by Trump, Farage and others. However, this thesis is false, in an era where burdensome government spending and regulation have increased the cost of essential goods and services, free trade and globalisation have been among the forces improving our living standards over the past 40 years.

The cure to sluggish growth and falling real incomes in Australia and the rest of the western world isn't a retreat from globalisation, but an embrace of the power of markets and incentives to reduce the cost of essential goods and services, while improving their quality.

*The macro environment*

The world economy has been dealing with two deflationary forces over the last 40 years. First, increases in the effective working age population, due to increased female workforce participation and populations in Asia and Eastern Europe entering the global workforce. Second, technological and digital innovations have produced significantly cheaper consumer surplus. The smartphone, for example, is a remarkably deflationary innovation, replacing thousands of services at a much cheaper price in a more portable and usable format.

These deflationary forces have been enormously positive for our lifestyles in advanced economies and lifted billions out of poverty in the developing world. However, central bankers have been pushed to the brink in efforts to keep inflation in their target range, or at least positive. By dropping interest rates to record lows, central bankers ignited a 15-year asset price boom. Homeowners and those exposed to share markets enjoyed record returns. Those outside of the housing market had to work harder to break in. This, combined with regulatory environments that have artificially inflated the price of other essentials, has increased wealth inequality and budget pressure on households, driving political dislocation.

Today, we are reaching the limits of the working-age population expansion of the past 40 years. Women are largely integrated into the workforce while baby boomers are aging out, the migration of populations in developing countries from regions to cities has passed its peak and developed countries are attempting to wind back globalisation. Covid-related supply chain issues initiated the current inflationary spikes, but more permanent forces will entrench inflation in the years to come.

Worse, this transition has arrived with government balance sheets in historically bad shape and economic dynamism, measured by productivity growth, at anemic levels. Three main drivers have contributed to this malaise.

*The professionalisation of politics*

The rise of sectional interests, abetted by the 24-hour news cycle, social media and the professional political class are driving risk aversion in policy design. The cost of adversely affecting one section of society has multiplied with their increased ability to vocalise their displeasure.

At the same time, the proliferation of professional politicians has reduced the risk tolerance of our decision-makers.

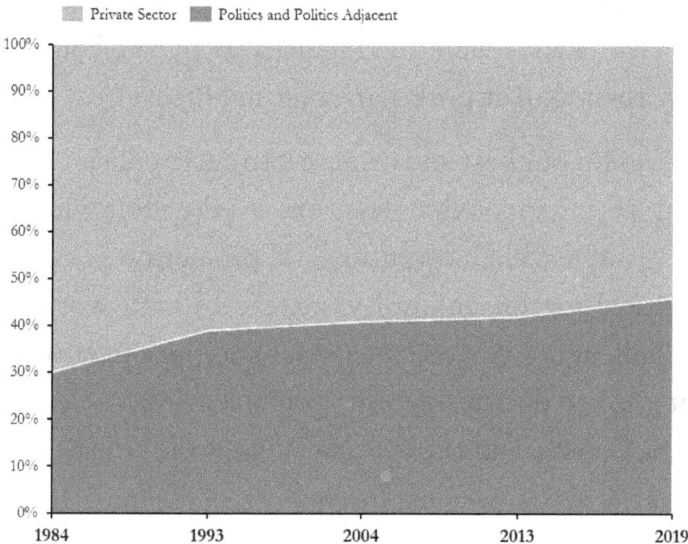

Figure 1: Professional background of federal MPs over time[56]

56  Analysis based on biographical information from the Australian Parliament House archives.

Politicians with substantial prior experience have a greater opportunity cost for service. If they lose an election they can return to their previously challenging and rewarding jobs. However, for those with limited prior experience outside of politics, returning to staffing or an adjacent field after being a Member of Parliament is a fate too embarrassing for most to comprehend. As a result, survival instincts kick in, and re-election and preservation are prioritised over policy achievement and the public interest.

In the commercial world, competing products and services vying for the same group of customers often trend towards similar features and designs. This process has occurred in Australian politics. After years of polling and focus-grouping the same voters, the two major parties have stripped any potentially unpopular policies, trending towards a mutually-inoffensive position. This peaked at the 2022 federal election, where the two parties were distinguishable by the colour of their shirts, their skill at pork-barreling and little else.

The incentives for our best and brightest to enter politics today are minimal. Trying to convince someone to take a role with low job security, intense media scrutiny and promotion prospects tied to political patronage/loyalty, instead of hard work and ability, is challenging. Anyone with a substantial career would be hard-pressed to pursue such an option, leaving a collection of careerists, egoists, and the occasional quixotic true believer as the stewards of our national interest.

*Global realignment of centre-right politics*

Over the past decade, centre-right parties in the western world have abandoned commitments to lower taxes and smaller government, transforming themselves into free-spending, protectionist/nationalist movements. In the aftermath of World War Two, centre-right parties brought disparate sections of the population together in opposition to trade-union socialism. This included capital owners, salary earners, farmers and trade contractors. This is particularly true in Australia, where the political system has been defined by the union movement, and those in opposition to the union movement, since federation. This divide makes little sense in a 21st century economy where trade union membership has dwindled below 10% of private sector employees.

This has produced an identity crisis for centre-right political movements that peaked with the election of Donald Trump as President of the United States in 2016. Trump's election carved out a new pathway to victory for centre-right political parties, winning the votes of previously reliably Democratic white working-class voters in outer-metropolitan areas who felt left behind by globalisation. This dynamic was replicated in the United Kingdom at the Brexit referendum, and Boris Johnson's 2019 election victory that dismantled the Labor Party's so-called 'Red Wall'.

The Trump victory and the Brexit election were shock results that went against the grain of mainstream media predictions and preferences. The emerging thesis was that centre-right parties could secure working-class voters and lasting majorities by eschewing pitches for smaller government and rejecting the 'woke' consensus. The angry white silent majority.

Social conservatives were buoyed by the idea that their pet interests could be secured, and economic 'conservatives' or rationalists could be taken for granted. It's not like they could vote with the trade-union movement.

In Australia, this emboldened the Coalition Government to reject action on climate change, confident that it had a 'silent majority' behind it. The Morrison Government deferred efforts to implement productivity reform, focusing instead on 'sovereign industry development': code for direct subsidies to manufacturing businesses in marginal seats. Scomonomics was the distribution of economic resources via the Mackerras pendulum. Economic resources were supplied to business owners based on how critical their electorate was likely to be for the outcome of the next federal election, not its proximity to customers, suppliers, infrastructure or the commercial acumen of the business owner.

Meanwhile, the right flank of the Coalition went as far as demanding large-scale subsidies for coal and gas power generation. Scarred by the 2007 WorkChoices election loss, and the political debacle of the 2014 federal budget's attempted fiscal repair, conservatives decided that economic rationalism was no longer palatable, regardless of its merit. Former Prime Minister Tony Abbott said there were "no votes in corporate tax cuts", while then Home Affairs Minister Peter Dutton called for the removal of GST from electricity bills as part of an ill-fated leadership pitch in 2018.

This backfired badly at the 2022 federal election, as the lack of contrast on economic policy between the Liberal Party and the Labor Party, combined with the Party's perceived shift to the right on social issues, drove high-income Liberal voters to 'Teal' independents in six formally safe seats. This gutted the Liberal Party of future leadership talent, fundraising capacity and ideological diversity. Stronger economic management had long been the core equity of the Liberal brand, something that was whittled down by a profligate administration more focused on wedge politics than on making people's lives better.

Economically conservative, socially progressive voters in Teal seats were unwilling to vote for a Liberal Party that represented neither of those traditions when Independent candidates offered them both.

### Sequential Tail Events - GFC, China, COVID

Over the past 15 years, the Global Financial Crisis, the rise of China, and the COVID-19 pandemic have placed successive nails in the coffin of market-based policymaking.

The GFC triggered unprecedented waves of economic stimulus from central banks and federal governments. The resulting re-regulation of the financial markets placed new constraints on innovation and risk. Central banks initiated quantitative easing distorting capital flows, inflating asset values and widening income disparity.

The rise of China as a global superpower has raised alarm bells over the integration of global supply chains with a potentially aggressive trading partner. This led to calls for the winding back of 40 years of globalisation and the re-shoring of major industries.

The COVID-19 pandemic doubled down on both movements. The ensuing economic shutdown initiated economic stimulus on a scale few had imagined possible. While the disruptions to global supply chains have encouraged politicians to demand a return to 'just-in-case' inventory management and the manufacture of essential goods at home, with little understanding of the potential impact on business profitability and the business cycle.

The lessons taken from each of these episodes are fundamentally flawed, and a symptom of the extent to which vested interests and risk-averse politicians are crippling our economy.

These three trends are undermining living standards across three key dimensions.

*Relative cost of living*

Over the last four decades technology and globalisation have placed downward pressure on the price of production. The cost of goods and services exposed to those forces has plummeted, while the quality of those goods has increased dramatically. Would you rather have a high-end television available 20 years ago, or a $200 television available in Aldi today?

Despite this enormous transformation, the cost of goods and services not exposed to these forces, and largely regulated, distributed, or subsidised by the government have grown substantially.

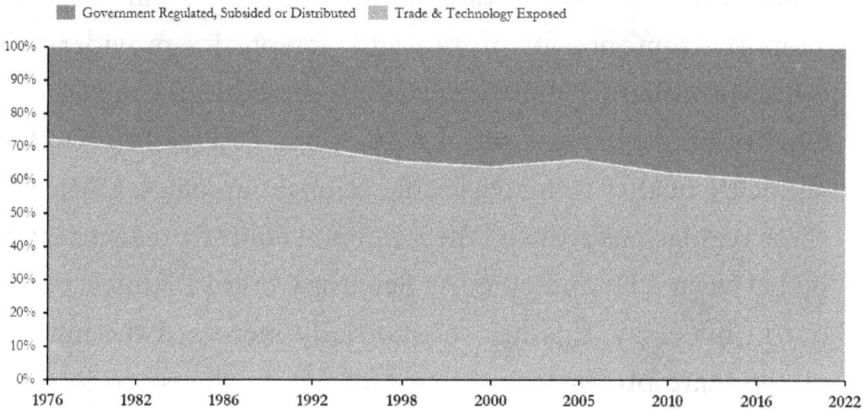

Figure 2: CPI basket components over time (%)[57]

The cost of housing, education, healthcare, energy and childcare have all grown relative to the rest of the economy, largely due to the government's inability to set effective consumer-focused policies. Childcare is a clear example of how well-intentioned government policy can have far-reaching and catastrophic economic impacts.

Affordable and available childcare is a critical element of any 21st-century economy. It allows both parents to return to work earlier than they otherwise would have, primarily increasing female workforce participation. Additionally, expensive childcare increases the overall cost of childrearing, lowering the birthrate. More importantly, affordable and available childcare is an essential enabler of gender equity and opportunity in modern society. The burden of child-rearing falls disproportionately on women, and access to childcare can ease that burden.

In Australia, childcare is managed by a complicated

57   Australian Bureau of Statistics. Consumer Price Index: Historical Weighting Patters, 1948 -2017.

combination of local, state and federal governments with support from not-for-profit, and for-profit, providers. In 2012, the Gillard Labor Government introduced the National Quality Framework. A set of regulations designed to baseline childcare quality to increase educational outcomes. Critically, these regulations reduced the minimum child-to-teacher ratios by between 25% and 60%. As Senator Gerard Rennick points out in his essay, this has substantially increased the number of childcare professionals, many of whom choose to join the United Voice Union, and increased the labour-input cost of providing childcare. Research has been unable to identify any discernable increase in educational outcomes because of these changes. However, it is simple to identify the enormous cost of these changes in overall price increases for consumers and additional subsidies paid by the taxpayer.

The productivity benefit of childcare comes from allowing multiple parents to deploy an economically valuable skillset in the marketplace, while one trained professional looks after their child for the day. The National Quality Framework reduced that productivity benefit, at an enormous cost to the country.

The social benefit of childcare, in the form of improved gender equity, is accrued by allowing a second parent to work full-time. To do so they will likely want to earn significantly more money than is paid in tax, the cost of childcare and foregone tax benefits, like Family Tax Benefit A and Family Tax Benefit B. However, this is not the case for a large portion of our population.

Liberal and Labor governments have been unwilling to take

on the United Voice union and the major childcare providers who profit enormously from the additional barriers to entry provided by the National Quality Framework, choosing instead to further subsidise childcare at the expense of the taxpayer and to the benefit of private providers. These subsidies are quickly chewed up by providers who have little incentive to keep a lid on prices.

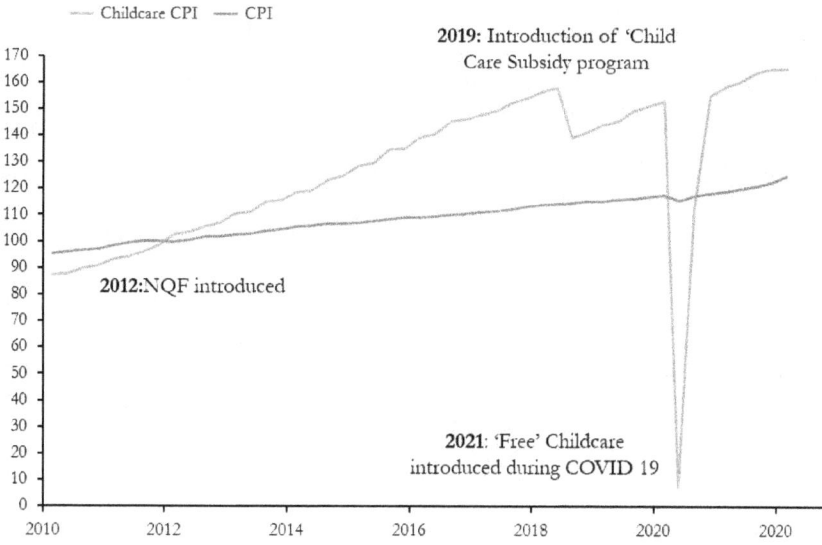

Figure 3: Childcare costs over time[58]

If government regulation and subsidies were channelled effectively to provide access to essential public services like childcare while leveraging the benefits of competition and technological advances, these sections of the economy could have avoided the cost increases of recent decades. This would improve living standards. A prosperous country must leverage these forces to avoid falling under its weight.

---

58   Australian Bureau of Statistics. Consumer Price Index. 2023.

## Security

The tragedy of this situation is that our economic capacity is being worn down just as our geo-political security is deteriorating. The war in Ukraine and the rise of China present the most substantial threats to the stability that has underpinned our national security since World War Two.

Our ability to respond to these threats is a direct function of the productivity and size of our population. It's not hard to understand that larger, more prosperous societies are better able to defend themselves than smaller, poorer ones. Assuming defence spending as a proportion of GDP remains at ~2% and Australia's GDP grows at 4% over the next 20 years our annual defence budget will be ~$80bn. If it grows at 2% it will be $53bn. The difference, $27bn, is roughly double the annual Ukrainian defence budget. That's an enormous amount of additional capability that could buttress our national security in these increasingly unstable times.

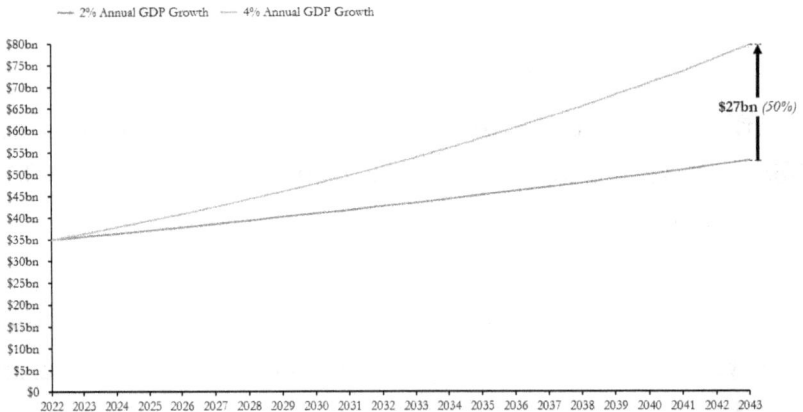

Figure 4: Impact of economic growth levels on defence spending ($bn)[59]

---

59  Australian Treasury. 2021-2022 Budget Papers. 2022.

Geo-political uncertainty, as outlined above, is likely to stiffen our economic headwinds, rewire supply chains and close previously open markets. It is no longer guaranteed that Australia can simply ride on China's economic coattails for sustained growth. We will have to look internally and generate increased productivity to continue to raise our living standards.

What's most disappointing is that the parliamentarians who have been the first to highlight the threat of China, those on the right flank of the Liberal Party, have also been the first to abandon the productivity-enabling reforms that would place Australia in the best possible position to respond to that threat. How can our politicians be expected to stand up to large-foreign powers if they are unable to stand up to the sectional interests sapping the life out of our economy?

*Growing government debt*

Our state and federal government balance sheets are in historically bad shape. COVID-19, and the inability of our politicians to say 'no' has sharply increased expenses, driving up government debt.

Since 2007, federal government expenditure has grown 8% each year on average. This has increased federal government spending as a proportion of the economy from 23% to 27%. The more resources that are sucked into government the less can be deployed by the private sector. If the government is not using these resources efficiently, productivity growth will slow.

The outlook for a potential reduction in the size of government is not good. As the baby boomer generation moves out of the workforce, the structural forces underpinning the federal budget will shift. The number of workers supporting each retiree, the old-age dependency ratio, has fallen from 6.6 in 1982, to 4.0 in 2020, and is projected to fall to 2.7 by 2060. Healthcare and pension costs associated with supporting an older population will increase. While migration can partially solve this problem, the political tide has shifted against large-scale migration despite the overwhelming body of evidence suggesting that migrants have positive economic impacts. Politicians are largely uninterested in addressing this dilemma as the consequences of inaction will be felt beyond the three-year election cycle.

Skyrocketing expenses have increased government debt substantially. Since 2007, federal government net debt has grown from --$25 billion to -$630 billion. After almost a decade of projecting surpluses in the forward estimates, governments of both stripes have largely abandoned the cause. This is a direct function of the inability of senior politicians to make difficult decisions. To extricate Australia from this situation will take an extraordinary period of economic growth (which could only be generated by substantial productivity reform), steadfast resolve from politicians to control the government purse strings or an extended period of high inflation. These options are either unlikely or undesirable.

Government borrowing for recurrent expenditure is a tax on the future wealth of the country. It will either be paid for by future taxation, forgone service provision or future inflation. As interest rates rise around the world, the cost of this debt will increase, reducing debt sustainability. The outlook for the government's fiscal position is bleak, a confluence of events and inept politicians have allowed entitlement programs to proliferate and spiral out of control. Demographic changes will exacerbate these challenges.

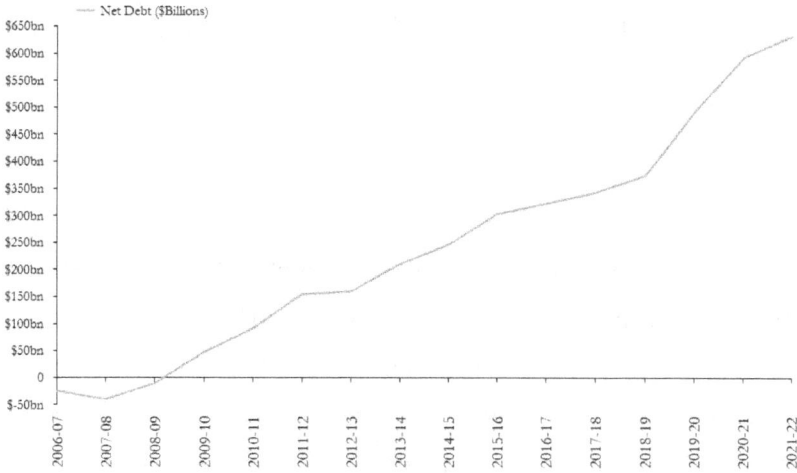

Figure 5: Australian Government net debt ($bn)[60]

The challenges outlined above are daunting, and our current political class has proven itself incapable of addressing them. However, there is some cause for hope. These are outlined below.

---

60    Australian Treasury. 2021-2022 Budget Papers. 2022.

## Business and technology

While politicians chase career longevity and positive media write-ups, scientists and the business community are working to overcome the challenges we face, whether it's the rapid decrease in solar panel costs over the past decade, the productivity-enabling capabilities of cloud computing or dozens of other technologies. These forces do not need the government to flourish but can be strangled if policy settings become too restrictive.

## Cure to stagflation

Our current policy settings have driven the return of inflation while economic growth sputters below the long-run trend amid the threat of recession. It was during the stagflation of the 1970s that free-market economics returned to the forefront. It is possible that a similar scenario could spark the political will required to rebuild such a narrative. The backlash against UK Prime Minister Liz Truss' aggressive tax cuts in 2022 suggests that moment has not yet arrived.

## Geo-political imperative

The short-term interests of domestic lobby groups appear increasingly petty in a world where geo-political tension turns to outright conflict. It's hard to imagine the Rail, Tram and Bus Union going on strike, or farmers demanding new and greater subsidies in such a scenario. The geopolitical threat to Australia may become so serious that it must embrace efforts to increase productivity.

Australia's position is not unique in the world. It has a diminished political class, substantial government debt and challenging demographics while facing geopolitical uncertainty and global economic headwinds. It is not a positive narrative. However, our country and countries like ours, have faced greater challenges in the past and overcome them. There is nothing to say we cannot do the same again.

*Harry Stutchbury is a Management Consultant at Kearney. He has previously worked as an adviser for Liberal members of parliament and as Deputy Director of the Blueprint Institute.*

# 16

# A new pathway to prosperity

## Tom Switzer

Since federation, the economic governance of Australia can be conveniently divided into three contrasting periods. Phase one, which featured industry protection and centralised wage determination, lasted from 1901 to 1983. During these years, the state was dominant in almost every corner of life and the economy was characterised by periodic crises triggered by external shocks. From Edmund Barton to Malcolm Fraser, every prime minister accepted the power of the state to manage the economy.

What the distinguished journalist Paul Kelly has called "the Australian Settlement" began to fray in the 1970s and collapsed in the mid-1980s when we experienced the currency and balance-of-payments crises. Australia, as then-treasurer Paul Keating warned, could become a "banana republic".

Australia was only saved from this fate by Bob Hawke's Labor Government. Showing political courage, he created a new economic orthodoxy, which liberated market forces, privatised state entities and slashed import tariffs. It was a Nixon-in-

China moment: when a political leader defies expectations by doing something that would anger his supporters if taken by someone without his credentials. In this case, the former union leader upset Labor's old socialist guard while winning support from his conservative opponents, such as John Howard.

The result was two decades of productivity-enhancing reform and, as a consequence, almost 30 years of growth with low inflation, low unemployment and, according to the Productivity Commission in 2018, no great widening in inequality. In real terms, national income per capita from the early 1990s to the peak of the resources boom two decades later increased by two-thirds.

Tragically, this second phase of economic governance ended during the global financial crisis of 2008-09. "Neoliberalism" had come to an end, declared Kevin Rudd, social democracy would save global capitalism and there was a renewal of the long-lapsed faith in the power of the state. Ever since Labor and Coalition Governments settled into what the Australian Financial Review calls "the complacency of prosperity". Canberra rested on the windfall of the China-fuelled resources development boom while it failed to curtail runaway spending projects (most notably National Disability Insurance Scheme, Gonski school funding, childcare, aged care, and public hospitals). During this era, the monetarist, free-market ideas that once defined liberal and conservative governance in Australia, the United Kingdom and the United States had been largely abandoned.

Even the right-of-centre governments of prime ministers Tony Abbott, Malcolm Turnbull and Scott Morrison embraced the political left's economic credentials as interventionists and big spenders. Borrowing was at astronomical levels. Incentive-sharpening reforms in tax and industrial relations to drive productivity had been shelved. At the same time, a debt-funded modern entitlement culture had taken hold, now tinged with the politics of identity and inclusion.

During this era, it's been widely assumed that virtually every problem confronting the Australian people is an excuse for action by the federal government. The result has been a productivity slowdown, wage stagnation and $1.2 trillion national government debt as the growth of government spending continues.

Australians have become used to relatively benign economic conditions stretching over the decades. But those days are over. With the Ukraine crisis, the global supply-chain disruption, the global energy shock, the fears of stagflation and the more dangerous geopolitical outlook, we have entered a new and dangerous environment. And although Australia's starting point appears better than much of the rest of the world -- after all, inflation and unemployment are lower here -- a lot of Australians could nurse losses in jobs, businesses and hopes and dreams.

What now? What should define phase four of our economic governance? What sort of attitudes should economic policymakers cultivate? And, just as important, what should they be careful to reject? Here are a few suggestions.

First, defend and prosecute the economic-reform agenda.

Australia demonstrates the success of market economics: from the mid-1980s until the mid-2000s, reforms to deregulate the economy and to expand incentives to work and save led to sustainable economic growth and higher living standards for ordinary Australians. So much so that until the Covid recession, Australia had recorded its 28th uninterrupted year of economic growth -- an OECD record. Far from leading to rampant inequality, sustained growth had delivered higher living standards across all income groups. Involuntary job loss as a proxy for job insecurity had dropped about 20% from the early 2000s to about 2020. To this day, and notwithstanding union scaremongering, casualisation in the workplace has remained around the same level since the late-1990s -- at about one-quarter of the workforce.

None of this is to deny the genuine sense of public angst about the pace of socioeconomic change. As Hansonism, Brexit, the Trump phenomenon and the wave of European populist insurgencies have shown, there are losers in technological change and globalisation. However, the forces that bred this creative destruction can't be stopped. As Keating and Peter Costello often warned, a nation that shies away from structural reform and fiscal discipline won't enjoy opportunity and prosperity for all.

Reform is a tough sell. But just think how the old Australia — the overregulated, highly unionised and inflation-prone country of the 1970s — would have coped during the global financial crisis of 2008-09 if previous leaders had not paid off our debt and implemented sound market policies to enable Australia to weather external shocks.

The lesson of economic reform is self-evident: jobs and growth are not created by state paternalistic power, but by private enterprises free to invest and innovate by being taxed and regulated less. If Canberra addressed the fundamentals of taxation, spending, regulations, education and the workplace, it would put in place the sound bases from which a long-lasting recovery is possible. Good policy to drive productivity and growth does matter.

Bearing all this in mind, any reformist government should liberate what John Maynard Keynes called the economy's "animal spirits" – that is, the passions and competitive instincts that are essential to economic growth. Slash costly regulations. Boost immigration to relieve inflationary worker shortages. Modernise our enterprise bargaining workplace system to drive wages through productivity gains without being eroded by inflation. Embrace an inflation-fighting wage restraint policy that helps avoid stagflation. Use the tax system to encourage entrepreneurship among younger Australians and help pay down the pandemic debt.

Second, vigorously oppose socialism.

More than 30 years ago, Francis Fukuyama posited the "end of history" thesis – that the collapse of Soviet Communism had heralded the triumph of Western liberal democracy and market capitalism. Today, though, socialism is resurgent across Australia and the Anglosphere. So much so that capitalism is regularly blamed for so much alleged doom and gloom: the supposed rampant inequality, economic insecurity, inter-generational debt, housing crisis and so on.

Millennials are lurching left in ways that could have profound consequences for Western politics. Since the beginning of the century, there has been a major shift in the political sentiments of young voters in Western democracies. As more people born between 1980 and 1996 have become eligible to vote, the political alignment of younger voters has become disconnected from the overall electorate. According to a Centre for Independent Studies/YouGov poll in 2018, 58% of Australian millennials have a favourable view of socialism, with only 18% having an unfavourable one. They believe government should have more control of the economy.

But no economy in history has benefited from socialism. All economies that have enjoyed sustained growth and have broadened prosperity have done so through free trade and free markets; regulation is the enemy of prosperity, and prosperity is the only means of providing the public services that socialists are so fond of claiming they prize.

Lower tax rates and lower regulation are likely to bring higher growth and help pay for some of the future education, health and welfare that society demands. Where do the critics expect to find the money in the post-Covid economy? You don't tax a loss; you only tax a profit. Without profit – without capitalism – you cannot raise the revenue to provide for these public amenities. The more business succeeds, the more the tax receipts flow into the Commonwealth treasury.

Australians don't think in terms of big or small government: as a practical people, we just want the state to act as a fair umpire that promotes individual freedom without creating an unacceptable level of insecurity. But there is also a long-run cost to dependency on the state, including an aversion to risk that boosts the entrepreneurial spirit necessary for innovation and prosperity.

Third, proceed cautiously on decarbonising the economy.

It's widely believed the world has resolved to reduce and eventually eliminate its dependency on fossil fuels and to step up its reliance on renewable energy. However, the timeframe most countries have set for this transformation is entirely unrealistic. As one of the world's most distinguished energy analysts Daniel Yergin argues, the shift to a net-zero world "is likely to take longer, to be more expensive and to require more technical innovation than many now anticipate".

The world depends on fossil fuels for about 80% of its energy. And in the 2020s, government budgets promoting the energy transition will be constrained by the heavy debt burden accumulated in the wake of the coronavirus crisis.

Accepting that there is at present a difficulty in achieving targets of net zero emissions by 2050, climate enthusiasts talk up the excitement of the technological challenge that the goal represents. They also claim that to take any other stand would risk affronting international opinion.

And yet as the West strives to cut its carbon emissions, the developing world – notably the two most populated countries on the planet, India and China – does not. Such countries account for 65% of global emissions, and they do so not to spite the planet or to offend the "international opinion" that carries such weight, but to try to raise their living standards as best they can. These are countries beset by poverty, under-achievement and, often, disease.

The fact is that renewables just aren't up to the job of powering the world's economies. Solar and wind power still provide just a tiny share of the world's total energy. They also struggle to replicate the reliability of oil and gas: today's best rechargeable batteries for renewables have only a fraction of the energy density of hydrocarbons from gas and oil; so, until this problem is rectified, there will always be a place for gas and oil.

We are seeing and will continue to see, the effect of the law of unintended consequences. The conventional wisdom is that the replacement of fossil fuels with renewables will lead to reliable and cheaper energy. However, reducing carbon energy has just reduced the supply of reliable and affordable energy, which means higher energy prices. Now, to reduce prices, governments are calling for more gas, coal and coal production.

Moreover, as former foreign minister Alexander Downer has argued: "How is it cheaper to have energy that has to be subsidised? If it has to be subsidised, by definition it must be more expensive. And the subsidies have to be paid for. If they're not paid for through higher taxes, then they will be paid for through increased borrowing. The increased expenditure and borrowing will contribute to increased inflation and increased interest rates".

Instead of the orgy of rhetoric designed to make noisy environmentalists feel smug, Western governments need to make proper contingency plans for their energy supplies and tread carefully in their reliance upon renewables: even if that means using coal to power generators of electricity, or the renaissance of nuclear power to keep the world's light on. And the developing world must have the same chance the developed one had, and make its prosperity as best it can.

One day, with market-driven technological breakthroughs, all this will be possible without using fossil fuels. But it just isn't possible yet, and we should end the pretence it is, or will be any time soon.

Fourth, normalise monetary policy to break inflation.

In response to the inflation surge in 2022, central bankers and their defenders blame higher prices on Russia's invasion of Ukraine and supply-chain bottlenecks that have disrupted the global production of goods. No doubt global factors in 2022 contributed to rising prices, especially food and energy. But it was the combination of vast federal spending and easy monetary policy in recent years that primarily set the scene for the emerging inflation crisis.

Until recently, the conventional wisdom held that, with interest rates around the developed world exceptionally low and likely to remain so for a long time, the heavy borrowing that had taken place in recent years could be cheaply financed. That helps explain why the Reserve Bank of Australia kept interest rates at near zero, even though Australia experienced a roaring economy and rapid job creation long after the Covid economic crisis had passed. The result of the extraordinarily loose monetary policy settings has been the surging inflation that has caught central banks and Keynesian economists by surprise.

The inflation surge has prompted a policy shift to tighter money: the RBA is now on the case, rightly raising interest rates; it will have to move faster in an economy that is still growing, but with less business and consumer confidence. Like other central banks, it has to find a way to reduce inflation without sending the economy into a sharp recession.

Fifth, repair the budget to help prevent fiscal policy from fuelling inflation and higher interest rates.

There is a widespread view that during the nine years of Coalition rule in Canberra (2013-22), the Abbott, Turnbull and Morrison Governments slashed spending on crucial social services. In fact, for more than a decade, Labor and Coalition Government spending on health and education as a percentage of GDP increased. And as my CIS colleague Robert Carling has pointed out, the program-specific risks of higher spending in the fast-growing areas of NDIS, Gonski schools, age-child-health care and now defence represent the largest threats to budget repair. Indeed, they account for about half the estimated total increase in federal spending over ten years from 2013-14.

But there is no such thing as a magic money tree – the belief that growth is natural, that budgets never need to be balanced or that money can be borrowed indefinitely to subsidise unlimited spending. The electorates currently so happy with free-spending budgets seem oblivious that the costs will continue to be paid by their grandchildren. But in situations such as this, it is not just the super-rich and wealthy who end up footing the tax bill: it is everyone.

For the moment, governments win popularity by engaging in this high spending, nannying management of populations. In response, these populations seem to suggest they like having others decide for them not just what they do and how they do it, but also how to spend their money. Economic history ought to tell these governments — and those who think they are doing such a brilliant job — that the usual result of periods of high taxation and high public spending is massive economic inefficiency, overregulation and suppressed prosperity.

The stimulus spending that led to rising debt might have helped Australia weather the Covid shock, but it was not a sound basis for long-lasting recovery, never mind the wasteful spending that distorts incentives and diverts resources from more productive uses. Without a broad reform agenda that sharpens incentives to create wealth, and without budget repair, future generations will pay for the high debt load with crippling taxation and a much-devalued currency. If the economy lacks robust and resilient foundations, it will become vulnerable to downturns, external crises or another black swan event.

The prosperity of the past three decades has made the Australian people detached – even complacent – about government. However, after a decade of quantitative easing and, in response to the Covid pandemic, massive fiscal stimulus, Canberra's conventional policies have been exhausted. We are entering new and terrifying territory. This means that there will come a day when our political leaders and policymakers need to exercise spending restraint and put in place productivity-enhancing reforms to grow the economy and pay down the pandemic debt. If they don't make the case for a classical liberal, market-oriented public-policy agenda, then the coming years could be grim beyond belief, with terrible consequences for each of us.

*Tom Switzer is the executive director of the Centre for Independent Studies in Sydney and a presenter at the ABC's Radio National.*

# 17

# Common good, not culture wars

## Chaneg Torres

The Liberal Party is supposed to be the party of individual freedom, free enterprise and growing opportunity for all. These values make for a good society for all Australians, maximising their opportunity to flourish whatever their background or identity.

But we must face up to the fact that the Liberal Party has been rejected by many Australians who would have a natural affinity with our values. The evidence shows that the fruit of a decade of conviction-light government has been a significant erosion in steady support and sympathy for the party.

Some believe the way back from the wilderness is to double down on divisive culture wars: to govern for sectional conservative interests rather than the traditional Liberal aspiration to govern for broad, mainstream Australia.

In this chapter, I address the view that the Liberal Party needs to be fighting a culture war to win elections again. Alternatively, I suggest that we must be seen as the party of the common good, not the party of sectional interest and division. I conclude that the Liberal Party, grounded in fundamental liberal values, can be the party of religious freedom, economic opportunity and social inclusion without contradiction if we are willing to do the hard work of cultivating unity and budling community.

## Who does the Liberal Party govern for?

Who are the people the Liberal Party needs to win back to be a party of government? Who does the Liberal Party govern for? This philosophical problem facing the Liberal Party in the wilderness of opposition is fundamental.

There have been strident and loud responses from the right-wing commentariat, with a narrow view of the party's base. It is argued that the true base of the Liberal Party is socially conservative on issues around religious discrimination, gender identity and sexuality, and passionate about climate change scepticism and coal-fired power. Thus, the reason the Liberal Party lost was that it did not take definitive enough stances on these issues. This was put starkly by the Australian Christian Lobby;

> The 'broad church' Liberal Party cannot survive long-term because it cannot be all things to all people. It cannot appeal to left and right at the same time...As the federal Liberal Party assesses the way forward from tonight's result, the Liberals need to pick their lane and reboot their natural base, which is socially conservative.

While social conservatives are certainly a key part of the Liberal Party's base, and without them, we cannot win back government, the Liberal Party has never historically sought to govern for defined sectional interest groups alone. The problem is that some commentators conceive middle Australia as a narrow subset of Australia.

The two greatest Liberal Prime Ministers, Sir Robert Menzies and John Howard believed that the Liberal Party exists to govern for a broadly defined middle Australia – the 'forgotten people' as Menzies put it or the 'mainstream' and the 'battlers' for Howard. In short, the majority of Australians simply seeking and striving to build a good life for themselves and their families.

Middle Australia is not just conservative men aged over-55 who live in outer suburbs. Middle Australia is broader. It includes the swathes of younger socially tolerant professionals, particularly women, who turned away from the Liberal Party. The Liberal Party cannot win them and win government back by only being a conservative culture war protest party.

The facts are these. The Liberal Party lost many of its formerly safe seats which were held when Howard was Prime Minister and whose government was socially conservative, but whose government had an attractive vision for broad, mainstream Australia through significant economic reform. By contrast, the Morrison Government went to the election supporting a religious discrimination bill (watered down, but approved by mainstream religious groups) and the Prime Minister even signalled support for the controversial Katherine Deves. Yet in the more socially conservative Western Sydney, the party experienced large swings against it and toward a Labor Party that had stronger climate policies and a more qualified view toward anti-discrimination legislation exemptions for religious schools. The Sky News/conservative commentariat thesis is further undermined by so called conservative minor 'freedom parties' not experiencing a huge uplift in their vote; the bleeding of votes from the Coalition to them was minimal.

Where the Liberal Party experienced the most damaging leakage was to the new independent 'Teal' movement. The issues the 'Teals' campaigned on; climate policy, integrity in politics, and gender equity, are hardly fringe 'woke' issues. The majority of Australians agree with these. Yet loud parts of the Party have treated these as if they were ideological issues in a culture war.

The arguments of the conservative commentariat reveal a mistaken false dichotomy: the Liberal Party must pick between two different bases. To put it starkly, they reject that the Liberal Party can be both the party of the LGBT climate concerned professional in Woollahra, and the socially conservative church-going working-class migrant family in Blacktown. In 2022, we won the support of neither of these groups. Yet the Liberal Party under Howard was able to hold a broad range of seats across a broad range of social demographics.

The conservative commentariat's purported solutions would have the Liberal Party lean into social polarisation, following trends overseas, where debates about national identity, personal identity (race, sexuality, gender, religion) and environmental issues are regularly fought in the public arena, often in a bruising and divisive manner.

*The problem with the culture war*

The robust debate over issues like religious freedom and climate change does not need to lead to ugly polarisation

– different sides can disagree yet accept when the political process resolves the (ideally respectful) debate through the process of election, compromise and parliamentary vote.

Yet now these issues feature the catastrophising of the stakes by commentators and politicians. This has been a feature of both ends of the political spectrum. On the left, we witnessed the appalling treatment of Andrew Thorburn, hounded to resign by an intolerant mob because of mainstream Christian beliefs his Anglican parish holds about traditional sexual ethics, and out of an irrational fear that he had secret hateful beliefs that would undermine his ability to run an inclusive club. This is despite his actions and words which demonstrated that his commitment to his church did not contradict his commitment to inclusivity for LGBT people at NAB and Essendon. On the right, we see commentators leaning into wild conspiracy theories about a secret cabal of 'globalists' from the World Economic Forum, and stoking fear that anyone trying to achieve a balance on climate and energy policy is in the pocket of 'globalists' working against Australia's national interest. They whip up anxiety around the Uluru Statement from the Heart, ramping up the stakes by saying it will create 'apartheid' and special rights based on race, warning that Australia will become perpetually divided on race while ironically contributing to that division by refusing to constructively work to find an acceptable model and unifying way forward that allows Indigenous people to feel in control of their destiny - surely a liberal aim!

Rather than respectful debate and seeking common ground, it is easier for each side to paint the other as mean-spirited, oppressive, bigoted and hateful. Victory over the other side must be won at all costs otherwise partisan champions warn that complete disaster will occur. Issues like religious freedom, dignity for previously marginalised groups, and climate change should be discussed with the aim of democratic consensus and securing liberty and opportunity for all. Yet when treated as culture war issues, positions are taken as emotional totemic identity markers of 'my side' against the 'enemy'.

But the loud and anxious voices of passionate activists on the extremes of either side are not reflective of the everyday concerns and anxieties of middle Australia – the true quiet Australians.

By contrast to loud activists on the fringe, Australians generally believe in a live-and-let-live attitude when it comes to social issues. Their votes do not shift based on these culture war issues. I suspect it is true that most Australians would be uncomfortable with the aggressive and intolerant nature of some radical gender advocates, but Australians also want LGBT Australians to be free to live lives of dignity. And so they feel unsettled by divisive debates about personal identity. I suspect Australians also want religious institutions to be free to conduct their affairs according to their own beliefs, but they do not want an ugly culture war played out in social and mainstream media that tears the country apart and leaves vulnerable individuals feeling alienated. Liberals need to support religious freedom and the rights of parents in schools as a matter of principle but framing these as culture war issues fought in opposition to an 'enemy' is a recipe for becoming a party of 20%, not 51%.

A majority-winning coalition of voters cannot be formed

on centring social and climate war issues. To believe that it can is to be deluded that Australia remains a conservative majority Christian country, or that a Trump-like homogenous disaffected majority in non-urban areas exists on the same scale as the United States. Australians by a majority voted 'Yes' in the same-sex marriage postal survey. More and more people are identifying as 'non-religious'. Australia has a high proportion of migrants from all over the world, has a more equal distribution of wealth, and is highly urbanised with an increasing proportion of tertiary educated people.

While I share concerns about the disintegration of a shared Judeo-Christian framework, culture war commentators must face squarely that you cannot do politics as if a culturally elite progressive minority have hijacked society against a socially conservative majority. The majority mainstream is not who culture war commentators think it is. The reality is what Catholic philosopher Charles Taylor expounds in *A Secular Age*, where the social imaginary is one that no longer assumes fixed transcendent meaning – belief and unbelief, and as a result, many values, are contested individual by individual. The question for a major political party is what to do with these contested social values. Do we copy the left and lean into a sense of victimhood and identity grievance for social conservatives? Or do we seek to build bridges across different groups and work out what is in our common interest? Do we, in short, seek to truly love our neighbour as ourselves despite our differences and disagreements?

Much can be said about the underlying causes of the aggressive and ugly polarisation we've seen, including the role of social media. But at its root is fragmentation caused by a lack of common unity bound together by a common civic friendship or love. Polarisation may feed off some truth; there is truly ugly racism, sexism and homophobia that exists in some quarters, and there is ugly bigotry against people of faith by radicals who wish to aggressively ram down relatively novel ideas about identity. But often these debates are amplified beyond proportion both concerning incidence, and the time everyday Australians spend thinking about these issues. They assume falsely that politics is fundamentally warfare: people with different views are enemies to be defeated.

People in outer suburbs still vote on bread-and-butter issues. They want a strong economy that keeps the cost of living low, where they and their families can find work, build a home and enjoy life in a secure country. They struggle to see how centring contentious social issues helps them with their daily concerns.

## Liberalism for the common good

Just as Menzies rejected the class war as false, the Liberal Party must not fall into the trap of fighting this false culture war as the central reason for its existence. Liberalism in the Australian tradition has always defined itself as the tradition for the common good against sectional and special interests, whether rent-seeking big business or coercive closed-shop unions. Today, we must not be the party of sectional and special interests whether they be religious interests, progressive identity political interests, or rent-seeking industries seeking protection.

As Liberals, we are concerned to preserve the freedom of the individual to flourish and to freely associate with others in communities that give shape and meaning to their lives. The goal of a good society are the things that matter: friendship, family, enjoyment, contemplation of meaning, learning, and a sense of place. These are goods in and of themselves that can be enjoyed by all and should be secured for every Australian; whether you think gender is fixed or fluid, whether you hold a traditional or more liberal sexual ethic, whether you are a tradie or a professional.

We can only secure these goods with liberty that allows people to pursue them according to their conscience, with prosperity only a free economy brings, and in association with others. It is liberty, grounded in a common sense of belonging to one another as Australians, that must be our guiding creed as Liberals. As these goods can only be pursued in community, securing the freedom of associative communities through which as Tocqueville argues the citizen learns democratic mores of deliberation and solidarity must be Liberals' social priority. We must be the party that seeks to strengthen those communities, though these communities may hold diverse views and be composed of diverse people.

We must create an environment within which communities with disagreements (such as traditional religious communities and the LGBT community) are not asked to let go of what makes them who they are, but are encouraged to come together to find a common purpose. This is the only way we can be a majority party of government, but more importantly, be a truly Liberal Government that governs in the interest of all.

We must resist participating in a culture war that says that Australians with different social values are the 'enemy'. This may be a recipe for strengthening support with people on the right who agree with particular totemic issues. But it is not a recipe for a party that governs with the support of most Australians and seeks to govern for the common good. A culture war on divisive issues will have no winners – and the debris it leaves behind is a culture wracked by division. The only resolution is winner-takes-all – a battle for power at the cost of the other. If Saint Augustine was right that a polity is united by common objects of love, the culture war can only bring unity through common objects of hate. Unity around opposition to a group. That is not the sort of society most Australians want.

If the Liberal Party is to be truly a party of government for all Australians, it must reject the politics of resentment and division. The goal cannot be to win power for one group to defeat another. This is antithetical to liberalism. A party truly worthy of government will govern in the interests of the common good. It will avoid the extremes and thereby avoid becoming a minority party. It will seek policy solutions that are for the benefit of all Australians, whatever their identity or beliefs. It does not lean into these cultural conflicts, pitting LGBT Australians against people of faith, or mining towns against clean energy.

While we have long criticised the left for its politics of class and racial resentment, the right has produced its versions of identity-based resentment. It should go against the grain of a liberal party to stoke bitter conflict and suspicion in society.

It's easy to draw battle lines and fight and divide, condemning fellow Australians who disagree. But we must not be afraid to engage in the difficult work of community building.

## Finding a unifying Liberal story

We need to find a story to which we all belong. But we don't have to look far. That story is about freedom. David Kemp argues convincingly in his multi-volume political history of Australia that the story of Australia is fundamentally that of a remarkable experiment in liberal democracy. Australia's prosperity is the result of its institutions and arrangements that reflect the philosophy of liberalism, allowing individuals to flourish in a land that values and protects fundamental freedoms.

The only way freedom can be cultivated and made to work for all is through the preservation of a united community. This cannot be achieved through stoking division, but through the building of community through the hard work of emphasising what binds us together as Australians and working out how we, through our diversity and differences of opinion, can flourish together. Indeed, national unity, more important than ever given the significant geopolitical threats we face, is only possible when people within the country believe they hold things in common.

Cultivating unity is a big challenge in the age of expressive individualism, where the alienated modern individual is so inwardly focused that they can no longer feel solidarity with those who are different. This is the danger of liberalism which does not also emphasise the importance of community building. Alienated individuals who do not practice living in a community with others who are different from them will more easily reach for suspicion and characterise those who hold a different ethic and who may disagree with them as evil.

Yet liberalism also provides the resources necessary for community building, because it provides key reasons why we should even want to put aside conflict and winning power simply for 'our group', and rather seek the good of others. Ultimately, liberals believe that freedom and dignity are owed to everyone by virtue of their humanity, no matter their sexuality, race, gender identity etc. A statesperson who takes seriously their duty to bring the country together, particularly a liberal committed to liberal democracy, must strengthen rather than weaken norms of respect during a disagreement because everyone is worthy of respect. With today's fragmentation, we must be the party that cultivates a shared sense of community, committed to the freedom of one another. A shared sense that all can belong to this free country, even during a disagreement.

To provide a historical example, Liberals committed to the common good did not let the prejudice of their Protestant base in the early 20$^{th}$ century prevent them from providing aid to Catholic schools. It's hard to believe now, but historically there existed deep prejudice and suspicion between both groups. Today, Catholics and Protestants still have serious theological disagreements; ones that go to the heart of personal salvation. Yet these serious disagreements do not now prevent civic friendship and cooperation between those groups. The real disagreements are not denied, but they are relativised when Protestants and Catholics meet in the public space to advocate for a policy that they believe is good for all. Now both groups easily find a home within the Liberal Party, because a good economy and freedom to exercise faith are good for both the Protestants and Catholics. They no longer see each other as enemies, and denominational conflict is mostly confined to civil town hall debates, not in the grab for political power.

There is no reason the change from hostility to civic friendship that occurred between Protestants and Catholics, helped by Liberal community building, cannot be the same for people of faith and people who have serious disagreements with them about sexual ethics and gender. Liberalism provides a way forward: to live and let live. To create space for one another. To live respectfully with differences while seeking ways to cooperate for the common good, with a fundamental commitment to the liberty and good of others.

How then do we handle deeply held disagreements? We must always start from the assumption until proven otherwise, that people hold differing views for good reasons rather than animus. A stance of charity and grace in our civic relationships, grounded in the love of neighbour as an individual with fundamental dignity, must be our creed. As an economic liberal, I do not think those who want more social spending are evil socialists trying to trample on my freedom. As a social conservative, I do not think all those who have concerns about religious freedom legislation hate people of faith.

The example of Howard in government is also instructive. Arguably he fought a 'culture war' of sorts. But in context, Howard saw himself as fighting a war against division Keating's

Labor had encouraged. Howard sought mainstream unity, rejecting the more extreme views about the nation's past, and saying constantly that the things that unite Australians are more important than the things that divide us. With this focus on unity, Howard managed to hold both socially progressive affluent seats and conservative aspirational marginal seats.

If we're going to learn lessons from this election, we need to reject the ideological nonsense of those trying to pit legitimate concerns about religious freedom, energy security and rural and regional jobs against action on climate change and concern for gender respect and equity. The Liberal Party at its best should be the party of religious freedom, low energy prices, economic growth, climate action and gender equity. To do this, we must undertake the hard work of building solidarity across the wide range of Australian society, offering policies that improve the lives of a broad range of Australians. While solutions are not easy, conflict cannot be our starting point.

*A party for all of us*

In 2022, the Liberal Party wasn't decimated in our heartland because of being too 'woke'. The Liberal Party lost because of a lack of conviction from the very top about anything at all. But all is not lost if we can find our way back again to conviction, believing, as Menzies said, in *"the individual, his rights, and his enterprise, and rejecting the Socialist panacea"*, and reflecting these liberal values in concrete policies that speak to the aspirations of all Australians.

Can the Liberal Party be the natural political home of LGBT

professionals and conservative religious migrants in Western Sydney? We have been before, and we can be again. Can the Eastern Suburbs female lawyer and the South West Sydney male tradie both feel that their interests are represented by the Liberals? I believe strongly the answer is yes.

Common good liberalism seeks to secure those fundamental liberties for all – individual liberty, free enterprise, free speech, and freedom of association. It recognises that securing these freedoms is vital to allow people to flourish and pursue the things that make for a good life. It also recognises that the things that make for a good life require communities within which individuals find identity and flourishing.

Yet while recognising the need for communities with real differences, it also seeks to cultivate a shared commitment and loyalty to the nation. It sees a place for communities with differences of belief to come together and seek ways of cooperation for the common good, without asking each group to relinquish their beliefs. This is a better way to the corrosiveness of identity politics, promoted on the airwaves of right-wing media just as much as the left. Identity politics seeks to stir grievance. Ultimately, it is antithetical to the common good.

In closing, I offer some brief principles for a Liberal Party seeking to navigate tricky issues yet govern for the interests of broad, middle Australia.

On religious freedom, we must not be seen to be the party protecting the special interests of some. As the party of liberalism, we must be seen to stand for the freedom of all.

This doesn't mean there are easy answers. There are deeply felt tensions in the community. Yet our role is not to stoke division and play off each side. Free associations and communities necessarily make moral claims on individuals that are felt more closely, and even above, the State. There will be inevitable disagreement between groups about ethics (including sexual ethics). True liberalism should make room for individuals to follow their conscience about these moral claims, but also cultivate a society where people with differences can accept each other's differences respectfully and cooperate under a shared sense of solidarity as Australians.

On climate policy, the change that economic transition brings must be concerned with ensuring that communities are not left behind. Policies from both sides of politics from the 1980s-2000s were concerned with equity as they also sought to transition Australia from a closed economy to an open liberal economy. We can learn lessons from that era and apply them to a market-led transition from a high-emissions economy to a greener economy.

On indigenous reconciliation, symbolism and practical solutions need not conflict. We should grab hold of the opportunity to walk together with Indigenous Australians and embrace the invitation given by the Uluru Statement from the Heart to put behind us the conflict of the past. We should work toward a reconciled nation where Indigenous Australians finally feel they have a stake in the Australian project and a say in laws that especially affect them (particularly given the race power in our Constitution). While we must legitimately debate the detail of a constitutionally enshrined Voice to

Parliament, we must not start from a position of suspicion, but one that accepts the generous offer of Indigenous Australians to *Makarrata* – coming together after a struggle.

Finally, we need to address the aspirations of young Australians. Liberals concerned about equality of opportunity and the Australian promise of reward for hard work should think it a scandal that young people who work hard will not be assured the same security that home ownership brings compared with someone who has access to family inheritance. Inherited wealth, not effort, is fast becoming the best predictor of economic security and wealth. Conservatives concerned about affinity and attachment to home, community and country should think it a scandal that more and more young people without home ownership will not feel they have a place where they and their family can withdraw securely and will not feel a stake in their local communities. We need to have the courage to tackle the necessary economic reform so that young Australians will have the same if not greater opportunities than the generation before.

There is a way through the perpetual cultural conflict, where we can learn to live with differences and share a common space. Not just as a truce. But where even with deep disagreements, there can be real civic friendship, love for neighbours, and affinity for one another as fellow Australians. It will take a Liberal Party willing to reject divisive culture wars and determined to be a party of the common good to bring this about.

*Chaneg Torres is a past president of the New South Wales Young Liberals and works for the financial services industry advising on regulatory reform.*

# Bibliography

*Jane Buncle*

Hurley, P., Matthews, H., & Pennicuik, S. 'Deserts and oases: How accessible is childcare?' *Mitchell Institute*, 2016.


*Georgina Downer*

Ergas, H and Pincus, J.J. "The Wealth of the Nation" in *Menzies: The Shaping of Modern Australia*, ed. By J. R. Nethercote, 2016.

Statistics from Department of Foreign Affairs, Japan Country Brief, 2022.

Menzies, R. "Opening of the ANZ Bank Building, Pitt and Hunter Streets", Sydney, 24 September 1965.


*Gigi Foster and Paul Frijters*

McLellan, S. "Chasing 'freedom' at the Federal Election", *The Spectator*, 2002.

Smith, A. "The Australian Government Guarantee Scheme for Large Deposits and Wholesale Funding (Australia GFC), *Journal of Financial Crises*, 2020.

Drew, M, and Stanford, J. "A Review of Australia's

Compusory Superannuation Scheme After A Decade", *Queensland University of Technology Discussion Paper*, 2003.

CNN Staff Writers. "Australia's Gillard cuts deal with mining companies on taxes", *CNN*, 2010.

Kohler, A. "Paul Kearing says Australians owed superannuation increase after being 'robbed' of real wage adjustments', *ABC*, 2021.

Cockburn, G. "Treasury concedes JobKeeper paid billions to profit-making businesses", *The Canberra Times*, 2021.

Chrysanthos, N. "NSW private schools reaped $72 million in JobKeeper payments", *The Sydney Morning Herald*, 2022.

Butler, B. "Banking royal commission: most recommendations have been abandoned or delated" *The Guardian*, 2021.

Fuller, R. "The billionaire takeover of civil society", *Spiked*', 2021.

Butler, B, "Banking royal commission: most recommendations have been abandoned or delayed" *The Guardian*, 2021.

Chrysanthos, N. "NSW private schools reaped $72 million in JobKeeper payments", *The Sydney Morning Herald*, 2022.

CNN Staff. "Australia's Gillard cuts deal with mining companies on taxes", *CNN*, 2010.

Cockburn, G. "Treasury concedes JobKeeper paid billions to profit-making businesses", *The Canberra Times*, 2021.

Drew, M and Stanford, J. "A Review of Australia's Compulsory Superannuation Scheme After A Decade", *Queensland University of Technology Discussion Paper*, 2003.

Frijters, P, Foster, G and Baker, M. *The Great Covid Panic*, Austin, TX: Brownstone Institute, 2021.

Fuller, R. "The billionaire takeover of civil society", *Spiked'*, 2021.

Kohler, A. "Paul Kearing says Australians owed superannuation increase after being 'robbed' of real wage adjustments', *ABC*, 2021.

McLellan, S. "Chasing 'freedom' at the Federal Election", *The Spectator*, 2002.

Murray, C and Paul F. *Game of Mates*, Sydney, Publicious, 2017.

Murray, C and Paul F. *Rigged*. Sydney, Allen and Unwin, 2022.

Smith, S. "The Australian Government Guarantee Scheme for Large Deposits and Wholesale Funding (Australia GFC), *Journal of Financial Crises*, 2020.


*Andrew Norton*

Bradley, D., Noonan, P., Nugent, H., & Scales, B. "Review of Australian higher education: final report", *Department of Education, Employment, and Workplace Relations*, 2008.

Cantwell, B., Marginson, S., & Smolentseva, A. "High participation systems of higher education. *Oxford University Press*, 2018.

Cater, N., "Demand-driven model devalues degrees", *The Australian*, 2014.

Cherastidtham, I., Norton, A., & Mackey, W. "University attrition: what helps and what hinders university completion?"

*Grattan Institute*, 2018.

DEEWR, "Undergraduate applications, offers and acceptances 2008". *Department of Education, Employment and Workplace Relations*, 2008.

DESE, "Student applications time series, PowerBI". *Department of Education, Skills and Employment*, 2020.

Friedman, M., & Friedman, R. "Capitalism and Freedom". University of Chicago Press, 1962.

Higher Education Standards Panel, "Final report - Improving retention, completion and success in higher education". *Higher Education Standards Panel/Department of Education and Training*, 2018.

Norton, A. ' The Coalition'. In G. Croucher, S. Marginson, A. Norton, & J. Wells (Eds.), "The Dawkins revolution 25 years on" (pp. 284-300) Melbourne University Press, 2013..

Norton, A. "After demand-driven funding in Australia: Competing models for distributing student places to universities, courses and students". *Higher Education Policy Institute*, 2020a.

Norton, A. "Disengaged and failing students are an issue worth policy attention", *Andrew Norton: Higher education commentary from Carlton (blog)*, 2020b.

Norton, A. "The rise and then slight fall of school completion and university participation rates in Australia and Britain, 1870s to 1970s", *Andrew Norton: Higher education commentary from Carlton (blog)*, 2020c.

Norton, A. "The social and political causes of increasing

educational participation from the 1980s", *Andrew Norton: Higher education commentary from Carlton (blog)*, 2020d

Norton, A. & Cherastidtham, I., "Risks and rewards: when is vocational education a good alternative to higher education?" *Grattan Institute.*, 2019.

Norton, A. Cherastidtham, I., & Mackey, W., "Dropping out: the benefits and costs of trying university", *Grattan Institute*, 2018a.

Norton, A. Cherastidtham, I., & Mackey, W., 2018b. *Mapping Australian higher education 2018*. Grattan Institute.

Sloan, J. 'There are options other than university enrolment', *The Australian*, 1 November 2016.

Stephenson, B., Cakitaki, B., & Luckman, M.. *"Ghost student" failure among equity cohorts: towards understanding non-participating enrolments*. National Centre for Student Equity in Higher Education, 2021.

TEQSA. *TEQSA's risk assessment framework: version 2.3*. Tertiary Education Quality and Standards Agency, 2019.

The Australian (editorial). 'Academic quality must be universities' main priority', *The Australian*, 2013, 3 July.

*Aaron Patrick*

Sarah Cameron, Ian McAllister, Simon Jackman and Jill Sheppard, "The 2022 Federal Election; Results from the Australian Electoral Survey," *Australian National University*, 2022.

"Home Ownership and Housing Tenure," *The Australian*

*Institute of Health and* Welfare, online article published August, 2022.

Aaron Patrick, "How the Liberal Party can return from disaster," *The Australian Financial Review*, 28 November, 2022.

Ross Kendall and Peter Tulip, "The effect of zoning on house prices," *Reserve Bank of Australia Research Discussion Paper*, March, 2018.

Aaron Patrick, "Mosman has a climate emergency, but no Woolworths," *The Australian Financial Review*, 11 December, 2020.

Peter Tulip, "An extra million homes won't fix the affordability headache," *The Sydney Morning Herald*, 27 October, 2022.

John Kehoe, "Boomers enticed to spend their home equity," *The Australian Financial Review*, 12 May, 2021.

*Chris Rath*

Australian Bureau of Statistics, *Taxaation Revenue, Australia, 2021-2022 Financial Year*, Australian Bureau of Statistics 2023.

Treasury of the Commonwealth of Australia, *Australia's Future Tax System – Report to the Treasurer, Part One Overview*, Treasury of the Commonwealth of Australia, Canberra, p.13, 2010.

New South Wales Treasury, *Review of Payroll Tax Administration*, New South Wales Treasury, 2018.

ACCI, *Board of Taxation Review of Tax Impediments facing Small*

*Business*, Australian Chamber of Commerce and Industry, May 2014.

New South Wales Government, *NSW Propoerty Tax Proposal*, New South Wales Government, June 2021.

Productivity Commission, *Productivity commission Inquiry Report: Electricity Network Regulatory Framework*, Productivity Commission April 2013.

New South Wales Treasury, *That's a wrap for poles and wires*, New South Wales Treasury, May 2017.

*Harry Stutchbury*

Australian Bureau of Statistics, *Consumer Price Index: Historical Weighting Patterns, 1948-2017*, Australian Bureau of Statistics, January 2017.

Australia Bureau of Statistics, *Consumer Price Index*, Australian Bureau of Statistics, January 2023.

Commonwealth Treasury, 2021-2022 Federal Budget Papers, 2022.

www.ingramcontent.com/pod-product-compliance
Lightning Source LLC
Chambersburg PA
CBHW052110230326
41599CB00055B/5525